THE WITCH'S BOOK OF LOVE SPELLS

ALSO BY
CERRIDWEN GREENLEAF

Mystical Crystals

The Witch's Guide to Ritual

Moon Spell Magic for Love

The Witch's Book of Candle Magic

The Magic Oracle Book

The Herbal Healing Handbook

Dark Moon Magic

Moon Spell Magic

THE WITCH'S BOOK OF LOVE SPELLS

Charms,
Invocations,
Passion Potions,
and Rituals
for Romance

CERRIDWEN GREENLEAF

mango
PUBLISHING GROUP

Cover Design: Morgane Leoni
Layout & Design: Megan Werner
Cover Illustrations: Alice / stock.adobe.com
Interior Illustrations: Alice, dbayan, Frogella.stock, Happy_
KrisMax, Maria Zamchii, mgdrachal, Nadezda Grapes, Olga,
ollymolly, PureSolution, Suesse, Tartila, WinWin, Ксения Хомякова

For permission requests, please contact the publisher at:
Mango Publishing Group
2850 S Douglas Road, 4th Floor
Coral Gables, FL 33134 USA
info@mango.bz

For special orders, quantity sales, course adoptions and corporate sales, please
email the publisher at sales@mango.bz. For trade and wholesale sales, please
contact Ingram Publisher Services at customer.service@ingramcontent.com or
+1.800.509.4887.

The Witch's Book of Love Spells: Charms, Invocations, Passion Potions, and Rituals
for Romance
Library of Congress Cataloging-in-Publication number: 2022944394
ISBN: (p) 978-1-68481-116-8 (e) 978-1-68481-117-5
BISAC category code OCC030000, BODY, MIND & SPIRIT / Astrology / Eastern

Printed in the United States of America

WE ALL COME FROM THE GODDESS AND TO HER WE SHALL RETURN, LIKE A DROP OF WATER FLOWING TO THE OCEAN.

—

I dedicate this to the elders in my family, who taught me the ways of the craft and how to know every flower, leaf, tree, and herb. My other wise women foremothers have passed their knowledge down, and we owe them so much. Love eternal.

✦✦ CONTENTS ✦✦

FOREWORD

Not since ancient Egypt has there been an entirely magic-friendly culture. Instead, all over the world, witchcraft and spellcasting have been victims of centuries—millennia!—of negative propaganda. To say the effects of this have been tragic is a huge understatement—it has led to oppression, repression, misery, and the torture and murder of those suspected of being witches.

This is not old history. Depending on where you happen to be in the world right now, anti-witchcraft persecutions may be all too relevant. The root causes of this situation are complex, worthy of their own books. However, to put it very plainly, aware that the spellcasting process encourages independent thinking, a yearning for personal autonomy, and sharp wits, authorities of all kinds—religious and secular alike—have continually sought to suppress magical practice. The misogynistic desire to suppress female power has also historically played no small part.

A standard negative stereotype portrays witches as cold-hearted, power-hungry, and malevolent, using their wicked wiles and secret knowledge to ensnare victims in their magical traps, akin to spiders luring insects into their webs. *Snow White's* Wicked Witch Queen exemplifies this stereotype. Witchcraft is portrayed as something dangerous and, frequently, like the witches' brew in Shakespeare's *Macbeth*, disgusting.

Au contraire! Nothing could be farther from the truth. Although there may be individuals who attempt to emulate these stereotypes, this is not the true essence of spellcasting, which is instead the desire to live deliciously. Spellcasting is built upon an awareness of the sensuous beauty inherent in our world and a profound desire to experience all the pleasures that life potentially offers. Cerridwen Greenleaf's *The Witch's Book of Love Spells: Charms, Invocations, Passion Potions, and Rituals for Romance* presents magic at its best.

You will find no negative spells within these pages: no coercive love spells, no vindictive attempts to cause harm, no malicious formulas to manipulate, destroy, or prevent love. Instead, there are spells, rituals, recipes, and other magical methods for manifesting, enhancing, expressing, and embracing love, including self-love, perhaps the most important kind of all. Simply reading this book induces sensual pleasure. Imagine the joy when you put the author's methods into practice. As Cerridwen writes, "Think of this collection of sex and love spells...as a sort of 'pillow book.' It is intended to encourage you and your lover to seek joy and intensity, revel in the heights of ecstasy, and above all, have *meaningful* experiences."

Witches are often understood to be those possessing deep, esoteric knowledge of Earth's natural mysteries. They are seekers and keepers of secret wisdom. You will find this exemplified within these pages, too. Cerridwen's chapters on the astrology, herbs, and especially the crystals of love are thoughtful, fresh, and insightful, and demonstrate her years of study and experience.

So, pour yourself the potion of your choice. Saturate your surroundings with love songs and pleasing scents. Adorn yourself as you will. Embrace your own strength, passion, and power. Let the spells in this book work their magic to help you manifest and receive the love of your dreams.

—Judika Illes, author of *Encyclopedia of 5,000 Spells*

Introduction

LOVE IS THE HIGHEST MAGIC

My first spellwork was about love at the request of a bestie. It might have worked almost too well, but it empowered me to believe I could wield the enchanted art. My foray into the path also came from an urge to help a friend. What better way to begin this process than with spells for love: spells that create the potential for love, draw the attention and devotion of a lover, strengthen the union between an existing couple, invoke sexual magic, heal a broken heart, and perhaps most importantly, fill your heart with love and compassion for yourself? Why spend a Saturday evening alone when you already know the object of your desire? And why doubt your power to attract love when a little herbal chemistry can make you virtually irresistible?

For maximum power, love spells require you to use herbs, crystals, and the right colors and timing with solar and lunar astrological signs with specific properties that correspond to your desired outcome. Luckily for you, we cover that well in chapter one of this book.

LOVE SIGNS: timing is EVERYTHING

If you want to strike up a conversation with the handsome, shy fellow at work, try it when the Sun is in Gemini, Libra, or Aquarius, the best times for communication.

If, after a few successful dates, you are looking for things to heat up, fix an aphrodisiac dinner one Taurus or Scorpio moon evening, the most sensual of times.

Declaring your true love will go well during the fiery signs of Aries, Leo, or Sagittarius.

If you want to rekindle a long-lost love, try Pisces or Cancer sun and moon when sentiments run high. As ever, timing is everything, and certain days are made for love.

—

Some people are born witches. Others dabble in the craft before they become aware of their innate power. For me, magic made its presence known early. Before I learned to read, I knew my astrological sign; by the time I was five, I had learned the medicinal uses of herbs from my aunt Edie. She was my mentor, and though she would sooner have called herself a medicinal woman than a witch, she was wise in the ways of magic. Like many others before me, love spells marked my entry into the practice. At thirteen, I cast my first love spell. Instantly, my best friend became the object of amorous attention from a previously disinterested suitor. Since then, I have had many years and ample opportunity to perfect this most joyous aspect of the craft. I have watched these spells kindle and keep love's passion alive time and time again.

The magic guiding the spells in this book is all positive, used only to bring light and love into people's lives. But beware the power of these spells! Avoid some of my early mistakes, like when I tried to help a girlfriend and ended up being pursued instead. I not only attracted undesired advances, but I also lost a friend in the process. The power you are wielding is no small thing; the more you practice, the more potent your magic will be. Becoming a good witch is easy. With desire, a loving attitude, a few natural ingredients, and a dash of magic, these custom-crafted recipes will cook up an exciting flirtation, enchanted courtships, and lasting love. I hope you and your loved ones will reap the benefits of this timeless wisdom. Then, in accordance with the grand tradition, pass it on.

PRACTICAL MAGIC:
PHASES OF THE MOON

Any good witch knows that the best ingredients can be found in your kitchen or backyard. Many plants now thought of as weeds have great healing powers and magical properties. Most of this book's herbs and essential oils have become quite commonplace. With the plethora of aromatherapy products now available, most oil essences and scented candles can be bought commercially. For the more unusual ingredients, try your local health food market, herbalist, or metaphysical store.

Performing a spell at the optimal time in the lunar cycle will maximize your power. As you read the spells in this book, keep this elemental magic in mind:

Each lunar cycle begins with a "new" phase when the moon lies between the sun and the earth, so the illuminated side cannot be seen from Earth. The moon gradually "waxes" until it has moved to the opposite side of the earth. When the moon has reached the far side of the earth, its lit side faces us in the "full" moon phase. It then begins to "wane" until it reaches the new moon phase again. The cycle takes a month, during which the moon orbits the earth. To determine the sun sign governing the moon, you will need a celestial guide or almanac.

My favorite is *Llewellyn's Daily Planetary Guide*. The moon moves from sign to sign every two or three days.

Chapter One

ALL WE NEED ARE LOVE SPELLS: CHARMS, INVOCATIONS, AND SHRINES

Any metaphysician will tell you that the most common request for help involves matters of the heart. Witchcraft is based on the knowledge that our destinies lie in our hands, even where love is concerned. So why suffer the slings and arrows of love gone wrong when you can do something about it? Magic not only influences desired outcomes but empowers one's self and fosters personal growth. This book contains secret recipes for aphrodisiacs, ritual celebrations for the high holidays of love, and insight into the mysterious realm of the moon and stars.

SELF-LOVE INVOCATION

It all starts with self-love. Here is an old saying: "If you can't love yourself, how the heck can you love somebody else?" This admittedly cheeky statement holds a lot of truth, but the bottom line is everything starts with self-love: your health, self-esteem, relationships, success, and happiness. Even if you had a less-than-ideal childhood, it is never too late to esteem yourself and watch as everything makes a turn for the better quickly. Making a daily ritual of this will weave this strand of personal empowerment into your life and make sure it is growing and strong.

Begin by sitting quietly, taking relaxed, slow, deep breaths, and wishing yourself happiness. After sitting quietly, begin to speak this mantra aloud:

May I be happy.
May I be well.
May I be safe.
May I be peaceful.
May I be at ease.
May I be content.

Continue this practice until you feel "full" of self-love and compassion. When you are ready to move to the next phase, think of another person you would like to give happiness and unconditional love to. Send the love through your meditation and saying these words:

May you be happy.
May you be well.
May you be safe.
May you be peaceful.
May you be filled with contentment.

CREATING A LOVE GODDESS ALTAR

Make room for love in your life and home! To prepare for new relationships and deepen the expression of feeling and intensity of your lovemaking, create a center from which to renew your erotic spirit—your altar. Here, you can concentrate your energy, clarify your intentions, and make wishes come true! If you already have an altar, incorporate special elements to enhance your sex life. As always, the more you use your altar, the more powerful your spells will be.

Your altar can sit on a low table, big box, or any flat surface you decorate and dedicate to magic. One friend of mine has her sex altar at the head of her bed.

Begin by purifying the space with a sage smudge stick—a bundle of sage that you burn as you pass it around the space. Then cover your altar with a large, red, silky-smooth piece of fabric. Place two red candles at the center of your altar, then place a "soulmate crystal" in the far-right corner. "Soulmate" or "twinned" crystals are any crystals that formed together. They are available at metaphysical stores.

Anoint your candles with jasmine and neroli oil. Keep the incense you think is the sexiest on your altar as well. I love peach and amber musk, which I love to smell. Your sex altar is also a place you can keep sex toys you want to imbue with magic. Place fresh Casablanca lilies in a vase, and change them the minute they begin to fade. Lilies are heralded as exotic *and* erotic flowers prized for their seductive scent.

Eterпal Love Altar: Dedicate Your Sacred Space

Here, at your magical power source, you can "sanctify your love." Collect your tools, meaningful symbols, and erotic iconography, and prepare for the sacred rituals of love.

Supplies:

- Red and pink candles
- Incense
- Victorian violet and rose essential oils

Directions:

1. Light the candles and incense and dab the essential oils between your breasts, near your heart.

2. Speak aloud:

I light the flame of desire,
I fan the flame of passion,
Each candle I burn is a wish
And I come to you as a witch.
My lust will never wane.
I desire and I will be desired.
Harm to none, so mote it be.

HEART CENTER: YOUR SHRINE TO LOVE

An altar is a place of power—your power—where you can make magic. It should express your deepest self and be filled with artifacts of personal resonance. Allow your altar to be a work in progress that changes with the seasons and reflects your inner cycles.

To create your altar, find a small table and drape it in richly colored, luxurious fabrics—perhaps red satin or a burgundy velvet scarf. Take one red and one pink candle and arrange them around a sweet-smelling incense such as amber, rose, or jasmine. Decorate your altar with tokens representing love to you: a heart-shaped chunk of ruby glass, potpourri made with rose and amethyst, or a photo of your lover. Fridays are the time for spelling love, right before dawn. Before you light your candles, anoint them with a love oil you select from the following pages.

Scent your wrists, throat, and left breast over your heart with the same oil. Jasmine and rose have powerful love vibrations to attract and charm a lover. If you desire sexual results, look into the flame of the red candle; if your desire is affection or flirtation, look at the pink candle instead. This simple spell, said aloud, will create loving magic:

> *Venus, cast your light on me,*
> *a goddess for today I'll be.*
> *A lover, strong and brave and true,*
> *I seek as a reflection of you.*

FULL MOON TRUE LOVE SPELL

To attract new love, two nights before the full moon, take a pink votive candle and place it inside your cauldron or any large metal pot. Lay a rose and a bell beside the cauldron and your altar. Use rose or apple blossom essential oil to anoint the candle's wick. For the next two nights, cup the candle in your hands and direct loving thoughts into its flame. On the night of the full moon, take a thorn from the rose and carve the name of your heart's desire into the candle's wax, reciting:

> *I will find true love.*

Light the pink candle and ring the bell thrice, saying:

As this candle begins to burn, a lover true will I earn.
As this flame burns ever higher, I will feel my lover's fire.

Ring the bell three more times and watch the candle
burn completely.

DAYBREAK LOVE SPELL

This spell can be used to meet someone new or to bring on a new
phase in an existing relationship. On a Monday morning before
dawn, light one pink and one blue candle. Touch each candle
with rose or jasmine oil. Lay a red rose before the candle and a
glass of water atop a mirror. Chant:

Healing starts with new beginnings.
My heart is open; I'm ready now.
Today, a new love I will meet.
Goddess, you will show me how.
So mote it be.

Lunar Almanac—Twelve Months of Full Moons

Many of our full moon names come from medieval books of hours
or from Native American spiritways. Here is a list of rare names
from these two branches of traditions that you may want to use in
your lunar rituals.

January: Old Moon, Chaste Moon; this fierce Wolf Moon is the time to recognize your strength of spirit.

February: Hunger Moon, the cool Snow Moon, is for personal vision and intention-setting.

March: Crust Moon, Worm Moon, Sugar Moon; the gentle Sap Moon heralds the end of winter and nature's rebirth.

April: Sprouting Grass Moon, Egg Moon, Fish Moon; spring's sweet Pink Moon celebrates health and full life force.

May: Milk Moon, Corn Planting Moon, and Dyad Moon, as well as the Flower Moon, provide inspiration with the bloom of beauty.

June: Hot Moon, Rose Moon, the Strawberry Moon heralds summer solstice and sustaining power of the sun.

July: Buck Moon, Hay Moon; this Thunder Moon showers us with rain and cleansing storms.

August: Barley Moon, Wyrt Moon, Sturgeon Moon; summer gifts us with the Red Moon, the time for passion and lust for life.

September: Green Corn Moon, Wine Moon; fall's Harvest Moon is the time to be grateful and reap what we have sown.

October: Dying Grass Moon, Travel Moon, Blood Moon, Moon of Changing Seasons; the Hunter's Moon is when we plan and store for winter ahead.

November: Frost Moon, Snow Moon; Beaver Moon is the time to call upon our true wild nature.

December: Cold Moon, Oak Moon; this is the lightest night of the shortest day and is the time to gather the tribe around the fire and share stories of the good life together.

Attraction Action Enchantment

I know this has happened to you, too. You met someone at a party, or you had a brief but meaningful moment in line for coffee, or perhaps you exchanged looks of longing on the train crossing town on your way to work. Now, your only hope is that chance will bring you together, right? Wrong!

Try this surefire attraction spell:

Take a man-shaped mandrake root (commonly available at herbalists and metaphysical shops) or any statue, photograph, or figure of a man. Place it on your altar and surround the figure's base with red and pink rose petals, then add red and pink candles. Place two goblets of red wine beside this arrangement and burn candles every night for a week starting on Friday, Venus' Day. Sip from one of the goblets and recite:

> *Merry stranger, friend of my heart,*
> *merry may we meet again.*
> *Hail, fair fellow, friend well met,*
> *I share this wine and toast you,*
> *as we merry meet and merry part*
> *and merry meet again.*

Make sure you look your best, as you will soon lock eyes again.

COLOR is MAGIC: A GUIDE TO CHOOSING CANDLES FOR YOUR SPELLS

This list can be useful when choosing candles for magical rituals or spells, tinting bath salts, or designing entire rituals around herbal products. Some differences of opinion exist, and color itself is a magical system. Use your instinct. Here is what each color represents so that you can select the right ones for your magical ritual.

White:	Protection, strength, health, energy, vigor, lust, sex, passion, courage, exorcism, love, power
Red:	Absorbing and destroying negativity, healing severe diseases, banishing, attracting money
Black:	Understanding, tranquility, healing, patience, happiness, overcoming depression
Light Blue:	Change, flexibility, subconscious mind, psychic perception, healing
Dark Blue:	Finances, money, fertility, prosperity, growth, good luck, employment, beauty, youth, success in gardening
Green:	Neutrality, cancellation, stalemate

GRAY:	Intellect, charm, attraction, study, persuasion, confidence, divination, psychic power, wisdom, vision
YELLOW:	Working magic for animals, healing animals, the home
BROWN:	Protection, purification, peace, truth, binding, sincerity, chastity, happiness, exorcism, spirituality, tranquility
PINK:	Love, honor, fidelity, morality, friendship
ORANGE:	Adaptability, stimulation, attraction, encouragement, all legal matters
PURPLE:	Power, healing severe disease, spirituality, medication, exorcism, ambition, business progress, tension relief

ONE MINUTE MAGIC: CANDLE AND CRYSTAL COMBINATIONS

Nature is the ultimate creator. At a nearby gardening or hardware store, get an assortment of seed packets to plant newness into your life. If your thumb is not the greenest, try nasturtiums, which are extremely hardy, grow quickly, and will spread to beautify any area. They also reseed themselves, which is a lovely bonus. Light the following candles, charging them with appropriate gems and stones:

- Green candle with peridot or jade for creativity, prosperity, and growth

- Orange candle with jasper or onyx for clear thinking and highest consciousness

- **Blue candle** with turquoise or celestite for serenity, kindness, and a happy heart

- White candle with quartz or limestone for purification and safety

Put the seeds under the soil with your fingers and tamp them gently with your wand, the branch that you should also stick in the ground. Water your new moon garden, and affirmative change will begin in your life that day. Get ready for the exquisiteness of new love. Ahhhhh!

WANDS ARE WONDERFUL: LOVE MAGIC TOOLS

Here is what you need to know about the perfect wand to use in rituals for romance:

- Almond is a sweet wood and smoother than many; excellent for love magic

- Birch is a wood that is powerful for new beginnings

- Beech grants wishes, so be careful what you wish for

- Rosewood is the ultimate

wand for spellwork, conjuring true, lasting love

- Lilac wands create beauty, harmony, and happiness and bring you love

- Ivy wood is related to women's mysteries and will bind together

HOW TO DRAW LOVE TO YOU: MANIFESTING RITUAL

The sweet scent of petals and herbs can bring love when you cast this spell. Try to perform this spell during a full moon.

- A small, lidded box
- 1 rose quartz crystal
- ½ cup fresh red and pink rose petals
- 1 whole vanilla bean, chopped
- ⅓ cup dried woolly thyme
- A pinch of ground cinnamon
- Piece of white paper and a pen

Mix the flowers and herbs and fill the bottom half of the box with the mixture. Then write five qualities you want in a new lover on the piece of paper. They should be a mix of personality traits along with physical characteristics. For example, a few years ago, I wrote that I wanted a love with long black hair. Sure enough, I met a handsome man with beautiful, waist-length black hair. This manifesting magic works! Fold the paper at least once so it will fit into the box. Fill the rest of the box with the herbs. Nestle the crystal in the herbs right at the top, then close the lid. Each night, open the box and take a sniff to remind you of your search for true love.

LASTING LOVE SPELL:
BIND YOUR LOVE TO YOU

On a small piece of paper, write the name of your would-be love in red ink and roll up the scroll. Anoint the paper with rose or amber essential oil. Tie the scroll with red threads, incanting one line of the following spell per knot:

> *One to seek my love,*
> *one to find my love,*
> *one to bring my love,*
> *one to bind my love,*
> *forever bound together as one, so mote it be.*
> *This charm is done.*

Keep the love scroll under a candleholder with red candles at the north corner of your altar until your will is done. Make sure of your desire; this spell is lasting.

WITCH CRAFT: DIY SWEET DREAM PILLOW

To secure lasting love from a nascent romance, a love pillow can cast a powerful, binding spell. This spell works best if you use a soft, homemade pillow.

On a Friday, take two yards of pink satin fabric and stuff it with the softest goose down and the dried petals of a red rose you've grown or received from your lover. Sew it with golden thread while you whisper:

> *Here rests the head of my true mate fair.*
> *Nightly rapture is ours to share.*
> *So mote it be.*

Anoint the pillow with amber and rose oil, especially when you "entertain."

BLESSED BE: HOUSEWARMING RITUAL

If you are not crafty, like me, you can bless your home by tying bundles of herbs to your front door. When you and your true love move into a new home, place a bundle of dried hops, lavender, or yarrow, representing long-lasting love, on the front door. Walk through the door, light your favorite rose

incense and a pink candle, and sit together in the center of the
front room.

Whisper:

House of the body,
We accept your shelter.
House of our spirit,
We receive your blessings.
Home to my heart,
We open to joy. And so it is. And so it shall be.

TYING THE KNOTS
OF TRUE LOVE

If you are truly interested in long-term love, this spell is for
you. This love spell may not result in a proposal and marriage,
but the rings are a powerful symbol to help bring true love your
way. You'll need:

- White rope
- 1 fresh red rose, with stem

- 2 plain gold rings (rings in a
  gold color are fine)
- Fine white sand (easily
  available at a craft store)

You can use thick yarn instead of the rope, but string won't do.
Tie a knot in the center of the rope around the stem of the rose.

Slide the two rings down the two ends of the rope up to the knot, then tie the rope again to secure them.

On the floor (yes, on the floor), draw a circle with the white sand large enough to hold the rose. Set the knotted rose down in the center. Sit to the west of the circle and repeat the following:

> *By this knot,*
> *I stir the pot.*
> *By this rose,*
> *the power flows.*
> *By these rings,*
> *my love I bring.*

Put your hands together and focus your energy on the rose and the true love you want to bring into your life. Repeat the words three times. Leave the circle and rose on the floor for one week afterward.

AN ENCHANTED LOVE LETTER

Love letters are an ancient art that always deepens intimacy. What heart doesn't surge when the object of affection pours passion onto the printed page? Magic ink, prepared paper, and magic wax will seal the deal.

Take a special sheet of paper (sumptuous handmade or creamy watermarked stationery is ideal) and write with a magical colored ink—red dragon's blood is available at most

metaphysical shops—or try the "Enchantment Ink" spell
that follows.

Perfume the letter with your signature scent or oil your lover
has appreciated, like amber, vanilla, or ylang-ylang. Seal it with
a wax you have also scented with one precious drop of essential
oil and, of course, a kiss.

Before your letter is delivered, light a candle anointed with
your preferred scent and intone:

> *Eros, speed my message on your wings of desire.*
> *Make my lover burn with passion and fire.*

Make sure you send your letter ASAP.

LET LOVE FLOW: BINDING INK SPELL

If you are lucky enough to live in the country or near a wild
and weedy meadow, you can easily find pokeberries. Though
poisonous when eaten, these magenta berries make wonderful
homemade ink. You can imbue this wine-colored ink with
magical powers with this simple spell.

During a waning moon, fill a vial with dark red ink and
add the juice from the crushed pokeberries. Add a few drops
of burgundy wine from the bottom of your love's glass and
one drop of a fruited essential oil such as apple blossom,
apricot, or peach.

Adventurous witches sometimes prick their fingers and add a droplet of blood. Incant aloud:

By my hand, this spell I have wrought.
With this sacred ink, I will author my own destiny.
And have the happy love I sought.
Blessed be.

Now write the fate you envision for yourself and your lover with enchanted ink.

LONG-DISTANCE LOVE: SENDING AFFECTION FROM AFAR

Perhaps you are in a long-distance relationship with someone special who lives many miles away. Long-distance magic can be quite effective, so try this ritual that has worked well for my circle.

Gather:

- A symbol to represent the object of desire
- Pink or red flowers
- Piece of paper
- Pen
- Small bell or chime

Take a photo of your beloved, a symbol that represents them, a gift they have given, or even

one of their business cards and place it on a pedestal or table.
Surround it with a small bell and a vase filled with one or more
of these "flowers of fortune," such as pink daisies, red roses, or
their favorite happy posy.

Take a piece of parchment and write your full name and
speak the following spell:

*On this earth and under these stars, I call upon the Gods and
Goddesses to bring us together and good fortune and the energy
of love to _____ [your friend's name].*

Ring the bell.

In this air and through these waters, speed here in the name of

_____.

Ring the bell again.

*Through the fire and through the rain, bring aid, goodwill, and
bright blessings to _____ now.*

Ring the bell again.

As a group, send the positive energy to your
dear one across the miles by saying, "I love you,
_____" and ring the bell vigorously one
last time.

SEEDS OF LOVE:
MAGICAL GARDEN

A great relationship can be cultivated, literally. By planting and carefully tending flowers that have special properties—like night-blooming jasmine for heightened sensuality or lilies for lasting commitment—you can nurture your relationship along. During a new moon in the Venus-ruled signs of Taurus or Libra, plant an assortment of flowers that will surround you with the beauty and energy of sweet devotion. A few of my proven favorites are listed in the garden of Indra that follows.

Before you place your hothouse posies or seeds into pots or flowerbeds, bless the ground with a prayer of health for your plants, yourself, and relationships.

Light a black candle to absorb and dispel bad energy and place it in the middle of a circle you have drawn with a stick. Dip your hand into a clay bowl of water and sprinkle drops behind you and before you. Sing out:

Great spirit, I offer you this petition.
Please cleanse this land—you are the greatest magician.
With my hands, I will plant and sow.
Here, a healing garden will now grow.
Blessings to you and to the Guardians of the Earth.

PLAᴨᴛɪᴨG EᴨᴄHAᴨᴛMEᴨᴛ

In all cultures, paradise is a flower-filled extravaganza. Eden was a virtual jungle; Kama Sutra lovers Radha and Krishna made love among petals, clinging vines, and scented trees.

Plants and flowers will infuse your environment with bliss. Cut flowers in the bedroom and parlor never fail to captivate. As a horticultural courtesan, your lover will come to appreciate more than your green thumb! Try cultivating a few of love's most captivating blossoms.

- **Wallflower:** Cheiranthus cheiri, "Flower of Fidelity"

- **Hawthorn:** Crataegus oxyacantha, "Flower of the Heart"

- **Yerba Santa:** Eriodyction glutinosum, "Flower of Emotional Release"

- **Cranesbill:** Geranium maculatum, "Flower of Constancy"

- **Honeysuckle:** Lonicera caprifolium, "Flower of Unity"

- **Evening Primrose:** Oenothera biennis, "Flower of Silent Love"

- **Rose:** Rosa, "Flower of Love"

- **Clary Sage:** Salvia sclarea, "Flower of Grace"

- **Periwinkle:** Vinca, "Flower of Closeness"

- **Ginger:** Zingiber officinale, "Flower of Paradise"

SENSUALiTY SPELL: FULL MOON GODDESS iNVOCATiON

At the next full moon, make a vow, alone or with your partner, to bring forth all erotic powers. Begin with a blissful bath in oil-scented water; this essential oil must be the one that makes you feel sexiest. For me, it is an equal mix of vanilla and amber, which I call "vamber"; it has never failed me. When I wear this unguent, I feel as if a cloud of sensuality surrounds me.

Sit in a darkened room encircled by flickering jasmine, musk, or "vamber" candles. Raise a cup of jasmine tea or a glass of wine from a vintage that represents a lucky year for you, and speak this spell aloud:

> *Now I awaken the goddess in me.*
> *I surrender to love's power.*
> *Tonight, I will heat the night with my fire.*
> *As I drink this cup, my juices flower.*
> *I am alive! I am love! And so it is.*

You will radiate passion and be intensely drawn to your lover.

TWO HEARTS BEAT AS ONE: RITUAL RUB

I always giggle when I see over-the-counter sesame body oil in the pharmacy. Unknowingly, a woman will apply the oil and never understand why she feels so much sexier and attracts more glances her way. While that marketplace version will do in a pinch, a potion you've made yourself will be ten times as effective. You can use it as a skin softener or massage oil.

In a cup of almond and sesame oil, add twenty drops of musk, sandalwood, or orange blossom oil. Shake well and heat slowly and carefully. I use a clay oil warmer with a votive candle beneath, but the stovetop will do.

While you are tending the concoction, look into the candle or gas flame and whisper:

> *My lover's eyes are like the sun.*
> *His body like the land.*
> *His skin is soft as rain.*
> *Tonight, we are one.*

When the oil is at a perfect temperature to your touch, pour it into a pink bowl and place it beside the bed. Tenderly undress your lover and gently lay them down on clean sheets or towels. With each caress, you will deepen their desire for you and raise their temperature. Tonight, two lovers will slide into ecstasy.

GARDENIA GODDESS
GLOW SPELL

Tantra, a greatly overused and gravely misunderstood term, comes from the Sanskrit meaning "ritual, meditation, and discipline." It involves a form of mutual worship of the Godhead (lingam) and the Goddesshead (yoni), in which divinity is achieved through a simultaneous erotic and emotional union. This exquisite approach to deepening the love between you and your partner requires you to share mutually held intentions.

At the nearest greenhouse or floral show, buy as many gardenias as your purse will allow. Ten or twenty of these heavenly flowers will fill your bower with sweet, seductive air. Place some flowers in crystal-clear bowls of water and some in a warm footbath and scatter some petals on your bed. Undress and light a single gardenia-scented candle at the head of the bed. Crush some of the petals and rub them into your skin and hair, then chant this love spell:

From the soles of your feet to the holy lingam
to the hair that crowns you, I will worship you tonight.
Love and God, on this evening, I share my entire being in ecstasy.
So mote it be.

Wearing nothing but one of the priceless blossoms behind your left ear, greet your lover at the door. Sit them in the bower bed and worshipfully wash, dry, and anoint their feet. The lovemaking that follows will reach new heights of sustained passion and spiritual intensity.

YOU ARE A GODDESS: AROMATHERAPY OF THE GODS

For men, this oil stimulates desire and prowess. In a favorite bottle or jar, ideally red or pink, mix the following recipe with a silver spoon:

- 5 drops rosemary oil
- 5 drops patchouli oil
- 10 drops yohimbe extract (available at most herbalist shops and metaphysical stores)
- A pinch of powdered ginseng root
- 2 tablespoons sesame oil

Use the oils on your fingers to anoint candles or massage your lover's body. For a chant or spell, you should speak lovingly to the object of your affections while you rub the magic massage oil into their skin.

For women: Follow the same instructions, but instead of the ginseng and yohimbe, which are greatly stimulating to men, substitute pinches of saffron and ground *dong quai* (also known as angelica root), long honored in the Orient as a tonic for females.

BELTANE ENGAGEMENTS: WICCAN HIGH HOLIDAY OF LOVE

This is the witch's high holiday of love, observed on April 30 with feasting and ceremonial ritual. The Celts of old made this day a day of wild abandon, a sexual spree, the one day of the year when it is okay to make love outside your relationship. After an all-night pagan lovefest, May Day is celebrated with dancing around a beribboned May Pole. You decide how you want your Beltane to go, as long as it is a fully sensual experience with food, dance, sex, and lots of laughter.

Ideally, you will celebrate Beltane outdoors. But if you are indoor bound, at least serve the food and the drink on the floor and insist on bare feet and comfy clothes. Serve an ambrosial spread of finger foods with honeyed mead (available from some microbreweries), beer, and wine. As you light incense, set out a few dozen white, red, and green candles and arrange spring's new flowers: daffodils and narcissus.

With arm extended, point to each of the four directions and say:

> *To the east,*
> *to the south,*
> *to the west,*
> *to the north.*

Then recite:

Hoof and horn, hoof and horn, tonight our spirits are reborn.
Welcome, joy, to my home.
Fill my friends with love and laughter.
So mote it be.

When your guests arrive, invite them each to light a candle of their choice and carve their secret Beltane wish into the wax. Ask them now to make an offering to the altar, which your invitation will have instructed them to bring: pink crystals, an apple for love, or perhaps stone-smooth sea glass from a beach walk. Sit everyone down to eat, drink, and make merry. Later, hand out colored ribbons and flowers to braid into other people's hair or around wrists, fingers, and toes. It will start getting markedly more *pagan* now. Turn the volume up on the music, though live guitars and drums are better. If your group is open-minded or of like mind, call a circle and invoke the randy May spirits.

MENDING HEARTS: OLDE WORLD SPELL

Sol and Luna,
the sun needs the moon like the cock needs the hen.
The sun and the moon have both hatched from the same egg
and represent the eternal attraction of opposites.

CALMING CURE AFTER A BREAKUP

To help heal yourself or a brokenhearted friend, add five drops of each of the following essential oils to a scentless base oil or almond oil:

- Wisteria
- Clove
- Jojoba
- Neroli

Shake and add a few small rose quartz crystals into the vial. Offer to give your heartbroken friend a neck and head rub. Dab the oil on their temples, neck, and shoulders, and gently rub in circular motions. Silently call upon Venus to assist. Offer the calming oil as a gift to your friend to use anytime he or she wants to feel more tranquil.

FRIDAY FRIEND FESTIVITY: PRAYER FOR PAGAN PARTNERSHIP

Perhaps you need a partner to support, encourage, and collaborate with in your magical workings, which can best be done on a waxing moon Friday night. Gather:

- 1 lemon
- 1 orange

- 2 rosemary sprigs
- Orange candle
- Fireproof clay dish

Group the fruit and rosemary around the orange candle. Light the candle and intone:

On this night
I do invite
new energy to bring delight
under this lunar light. So mote it be.

Now, using the candle flame, light the tips of the rosemary twigs and set them in the dish. Rosemary is a powerful cleansing smoke used as an incense by ancient priests and priestesses in Greek and Roman times and by prophets and seers. It cleanses the aura and paves the way for major magic. Soon your partner in spellwork will appear.

HEAL YOUR HEART CHARM

The Friday before the new moon—Venus' Day—is the perfect time to create a new opportunity and clear away relationship "baggage." Place a bowl of water on your altar. Light two rose-scented pink candles and a gardenia or vanilla-scented white candle. Burn amber incense in between the candles. Sprinkle salt on your altar cloth and ring a bell, then recite aloud:

Hurt and pain are banished this night;
fill this heart and home with light.

Ring the bell again. Toss the bowl of water out your front door, and love troubles should drain away.

MONDAY MORNING SPELL FOR NEW BEGINNINGS

This spell can be used to meet someone new or to bring on a new phase in an existing relationship. On a Monday morning before dawn, light one pink and one blue candle. Touch each candle with lily, freesia, or jasmine oil. Lay a lily on your altar with some catnip. Place a lapis lazuli stone in front of the lily and a glass of water atop a mirror. Chant:

> *Healing starts with new beginnings.*
> *My heart is open; I'm ready now.*
> *Today, a new love I will meet.*
> *Goddess, you will show me how.*
> *So mote it be.*

Drink a cup of hot honeyed cinnamon tea that you stirred counterclockwise with a cinnamon stick. Sprinkle the powdered version of this charismatic spice on the threshold of your front door and along your entry path. When the cinnamon powder is crushed underfoot, its regenerative powers will help you start a fresh chapter in your love life.

WANING MOON
MOVING ON SPELL

Most of us have had problems giving up on a relationship. This ritual will help you let go. Perform this ritual during the waning moon when things can best be put to rest. Gather:

- Black string
- A symbol of your ex
- Scissors

Tie the black string around your waist and attach it to the symbol of your ex: a photo, a memento, or a lock of hair. Take the pair of scissors in your hand, and prepare to use them by saying:

Bygones be and lovers part,
I'm asking you to leave my heart.
Go in peace, harm to none.
My new life is begun.

Cut the string and toss away the memento. You will feel freer and lighter immediately and will begin to attract many new potential paramours.

A Witch's Calendar

January 6: Feast of Sirona, the blessing of the waters

January 11: Carmentalia, a woman's festival celebrating midwifery and birth

February 2: Candlemas, when new witches are initiated with the waxing of winter light

February 14: Aphrodite's Week, a festival of love (now Valentine's Day)

March 20: Vernal Equinox, when the mythological maiden returns from underground with spring

March 30: Feast of Fertility, a rite of spring for planting and sowing

April 28: Festival of Flora, rituals of abundance for new flowers and vegetables

May 1: Beltane, pagan feasting and mating ceremonies to mark the approach of summer

June 1: Festival of Epipi, an explanation of the Full Moon and her mysteries

June 7: Vestalia, the Feast of Vesta, the Greek goddess of home and hearth

June 21: Summer Solstice, when fire circles honor Midsummer—the longest day

July 7: Nonae Carpotinae, an ancient Roman custom celebrating women with feasts under the fig tree

July 17: Isis Day, when the Egyptian goddess queen is honored and embodied

August 2: Lammas Day, a ritual of remembrance for Earth Mother and Fortuna

August 13: Festival for Diana, the huntress moon goddess, who is worshipped with fires and pilgrimages

August 21: Consualia, greeting the coming harvest with dances, feasting, song, and contests of speed and strength

September 23: Autumnal Equinox, the pagan time for giving thanks

October 31: Hallowmas, the witch's New Year, when the veil between worlds is thinnest

December 19: Opalia observes Ops, the ancient goddess of farmers and fertility

December 21: Winter Solstice, the shortest day

WITCH CRAFT: HERBAL WREATH

Often, your kitchen is the heart of the home. Something about cooking and sharing food brings people together. An herbal wreath hanging on the kitchen door can be a source of love and luck. You'll need the following for your creation:

- Freshly cut herbs of your choice
- A wire wreath frame, available from most craft stores
- Either string or florist's wire, ribbon, and perhaps a hot glue gun

This is truly one of the simplest craft projects you can make. Just utilize the wreath frame as a base, and use string or the florist's wire to anchor the fresh herbs into place. Finish it with a colorful ribbon or other magical decorative touches you may want to add.

HEART WREATH

Don't wait until Valentine's Day to try this; love should be twenty-four seven, 365 days a year. Invite love into your home by hanging a wreath full of love herbs on your door. Any combination of these will work beautifully and I recommend using herbs that personally resonate with you among these options: allspice, clove, catnip, fig, bleeding heart, periwinkle, tulip, peppermint, violet, daffodil, lavender, and marjoram. Adorn with pink and red ribbons to let the universe know you're ready to welcome love into your life.

Chapter Two

ELIXIR OF LOVE: PASSION POTIONS AND LOVING LIBATIONS

here are elixirs, love potions, and many luscious libations in this chapter that you will enjoy with loved ones, a special someone, or your soul tribe. I have gone out of my way to make sure they are organic and healthy options with magical qualities for much merriment. Even herbal tea can support an enchanted life filled with love. Many enthusiasts enjoy several cups a day of their favorite herbal infusion; made strong, it is a large portion of herbs brewed for at least four hours and even as long as ten. I recommend placing one cup of the dried herb into a quart canning jar and filling it with freshly boiled water. Make sure to put a large metal spoon or a butter knife in the jar first so that the heat will not crack the glass. After the steeping, strain with a nonmetallic strainer, such as cheesecloth or a bamboo strainer basket. Herbal infusions can be made with leaves and fruits, which give healing qualities to this comforting brew. Many favorite kitchen garden herbs contain minerals, antioxidants, and phytochemicals, including the list herein.

TEA FOR TWO: MAGICAL PROPERTIES OF HERBAL TEA

What do you need to transform in your life now? This list of herbs and associations can be your guide; one of the smartest ways to approach this methodology is to brew right before bedtime. You will awaken to a freshly infused herb. Some of the most popular herbs and fruits used to create infusions are as follows:

- Anise Seeds and Leaves: soothing for cramps and aches

- Caraway Seeds: aid in romantic issues, helps with colic

- Catnip Leaves: make women even more attractive

- **Chamomile Flowers:** help with sleep, good for abundance

- Dandelion Leaves: make wishes come true

- Echinacea: makes the body strong

- Ginseng Root: increases men's vigor

- Nettle Leaves: lung function, hex breaking

- **Peppermint Leaves:** clear tummy discomfort, cleansing

- Pine Needles: increase skin health as well as financial health

- Rose Hip Fruit: packed with vitamin C and can halt colds and flu

- Sage Leaves: purify energy, antibiotic

- Skullcap Leaves: prevent insomnia and soothe nerves

- **St. John's Wort:** antidepressant

- Thyme Leaves: antiseptic, a protectant

- Yarrow Flowers: reduce fever, bring courage and good luck

HERBAL ELIXIR: BREW OF †HE BELOVED

Here's a quick recipe to create exactly the right mood for a romantic evening.

Stir together in a clockwise motion:

- 1 ounce dried hibiscus flowers

- 1 ounce dried and pulverized rose hips

- ½ ounce dried lemon balm

- ½ ounce dried mint (ideally peppermint)

- ½ ounce meadowsweet

Store this herbal concoction in a dark, lidded jar or tin. (It will keep for one year, after which you can recycle the herbs as a blessing for the hearth fire.)

When you are ready to brew the tea, pick your most sacred teapot and pour boiling water over the herbs; use two teaspoons for each cup of water. Say the following spell aloud during the five minutes it takes for the tea to steep, and visualize your heart's desire:

Herbal brew of love's emotion,
with my wish I fortify.
When two people share this potion,
their love shall intensify
as in the Olde Garden of Love.

Sweeten to taste with honey and share this luscious *libation* with the one you *love*.

GETTING HYGGE WITH YOUR HONEY: HERBAL BREW

We might call it kitchen witchery and our Scandinavian friends could say it is how we "get hygge," which means to get as cozy as humanly possible. This newly trendy lifestyle tradition from the frozen north is not just for lazing about, though we greatly appreciate that aspect; it is also a healthy way of living with sauna sessions, lots of herbal food and drink but also with your sweetheart, which is an immunity booster on its own. Tea is a mainstay if you want to be comfy and doze, and we feel sure wise women and hedge witches in Northern Europe were the first on the hygge bandwagon. For an ambrosial brew you can enjoy together, add a sliver of ginger root and a pinch each of echinacea and mint to a cup of hot black tea. Add a teaspoon of honey. Now relax and enjoy!

TRUE LOVE TEA

Here's a recipe to create exactly the right mood for romance. The verse at the end references the Garden of Eden before the fall. Gather the following:

- 1 ounce dried hibiscus flowers
- 1 ounce dried and pulverized rose hips
- ½ ounce dried lemon balm
- ½ ounce dried mint (ideally peppermint)
- ½ ounce dried meadowsweet

Stir ingredients together in a clockwise motion. Store in a dark, lidded jar.

To make tea, add two teaspoons of herbs for each cup of boiled water. Steep for five minutes while visualizing your heart's desire, and before straining, say aloud:

> *Herbal brew of love's emotion,*
> *with my wish I fortify.*
> *When two people share this potion*

their love shall intensify
as in the Olde Garden of Love.

READ THE TEA LEAVES

After sipping your tea, let the leaves guide you to your lover's lair. The answer to *where* you should make love lies at the bottom of the cup.

As you study the leaves, keep in mind that the teacup handle is south, and going clockwise around the circle, the left is west, the top is north, and the east is to the right of the handle when the handle is toward you.

- North, you should tryst outside
- West, you should go to your bedroom
- South is in the kitchen or living room
- East is at your lover's house

PASSION POTION: TEA FOR TWO

A tea of mandrake root, when mixed with the sweat of a lover, can be sprinkled around the bedroom to heighten ecstasy if accompanied by this chant:

Brew of mandrake, brew of desire,
enchant this bed with passion's fire.
Cast a spell of ecstasy.
This is my will. So mote it be.

Infused with Love: Lavender Rosemary Libation

This clear alcoholic drink is easily infused with the flavor of flowers, herbs, fruits, and even vegetables. Try combinations such as the light and sweet floral taste of lavender and rosemary. Lavender brings calming and healing and rosemary dispels negative spirits. Both are love herbs. What could be better? You'll need the following:

- 1 quart bottle of vodka
- 2 sprigs of rosemary
- 3 sprigs of lavender
- Large canning jar with sealable lid

After you have rinsed your herbs in cool water and gently patted them dry, put them in the one-quart (or thirty-two-ounce) Mason or Bell jar. Pour in vodka, making sure to cover the herbs to the top and seal tightly. Give it a vigorous shake and place in your pantry or dark closet for five days, making sure to shake at least once a day. After the second day, take a spoon and taste the vodka. If the taste suits you before the full five days, strain the herbs out using a cheesecloth or a paper coffee filter. Set the herbs aside and let them dry. After the vodka is thoroughly strained of any herbs or residue, pour it into a bottle and label it with the date and the herbs used. Tie the dry herbs into a bundle with string and use when you next make a fire in the hearth. The scentful smoke will imbue your home with coziness, calm, healing, and love.

BLISS BREW: APRICOT PASSION POTION

This witch's brew is intended to enhance the expression of passion, as its name foretells. Upon imbibing the drink and indulging in erotic exploits, mutual orgasms are guaranteed. You will need the following:

- ⅓ cup dried vervain
- 9 dried apricots
- Honey
- Brandy
- Glass decanter
- Mortar and pestle

Using a mortar and pestle, grind the dried vervain to a powder—hemp can also be added or substituted if you're inclined.

Dip the nine dried apricots in honey, then roll them in the powder you've just made. Steep the apricots in one cup of your best brandy and store in a tightly sealed glass decanter.

Store the cordial in a cool, dark place for one complete moon cycle. Whenever you have an erotic thought, shake the potion while fantasizing about mind-blowing sex. Consult your moon calendar and wait until the moon is in Cancer, Pisces, or Scorpio before straining and serving. Drink, and total bliss is yours for the asking.

Sweet Potion for Sharing: Lunar Libation

For a passionate pick-me-up, drink this tasty tea with your lover.

In a pint of distilled or spring water, heat the root of ginseng for no less than an hour. Simmer, don't boil, cover, and don't dare stir. Pour yourself a cup for love's sure power.

Before you drink this lustful libation, simply say:

Gift of the goddess and magic of moon,
may the flower of our love come to full bloom.

Shared between two lovers before a tryst, this enchanted potion will give great endurance for a memorable encounter.

BEWITCHING BREW: APPLE BRANDY SPIRITS

Here is a delightfully easy recipe that will produce a flavorful homemade liqueur that smells as good as it tastes. If you are interested in making a hassle-free bottle of special spirits, apples are a wonderful way to start. Start with these ingredients:

- 4 apples (sweet, not sour)
- 2 cups brandy
- 2 cups vodka
- Clean and sterilized one-quart Mason jar

First, clean, core, and slice your apples. Place the slices in a Mason canning jar. Pour in the alcohol to cover, using equal parts brandy and vodka. Put the jar in a cool, dark place in your pantry. Allow the infusion process to happen for a month or until it is to your taste. The combination of sweet apples and brandy yields a luscious fruit-forward flavor with no need for sugar. After infusing, strain the apple slices using a strainer to filter the liqueur. Pour the spirits into a pretty and sealable bottle and enjoy at your next pagan party. (The apple slices can be eaten—but bear in mind that though it may not taste like it, there will probably be a significant amount of liquor in the strained-out fruit!)

Bonus tip: apples can be used with any spirit, so let your imagination run wild!

The Enchanted Orchard: Fruit Magic

While we often think of herbs and flowers as having special properties, it is much less commonly known that fruits also contain much magic you must try for yourself:

Apples: This beloved "one a day" fruit is associated with the goddess Pomona and contains the powers of healing, love, and abundance. Samhain, the high holiday of the Wheel of the Year, is also called the "Feast of Apples," and they are used on the Halloween altar during this festival. Cutting an apple in half and sharing the other half with your beloved will generate magic so that the two of you will stay happy.

Apricots: This juicy treasure is associated with Venus and the power of love, and it is believed that drinking the nectar will make you more romantically appealing. The juice of the apricot is used in rituals and love potions. Truly a food of the goddess!

Avocados: Not only is the luscious avocado is not just delicious, it also brings forth beauty and lustfulness.

Bananas: A bunch of bananas packs a magical punch with powers of abundance and fertility for both men and women. Anyone who gets married beneath a banana tree bower will have a lucky marriage. One caveat: never cut a banana; only break the fruit apart. Otherwise, you'll bring bad luck to your household.

Blackberries: Blackberries are the medicine that pops up anywhere, offering a delightful snack and serious healing, love, and abundance. Both the vine and the berries can be used for money-bringing spells. Thorny blackberry vines are wonderful as protective wreaths for your home, and the plant vine and the berry can be used for prosperity and money spells.

Blueberries: These berries are almost like a shield against the evil eye made of fruit, as they offer great protection. You can tuck them under the mat at your front threshold to ward off bad energy and evil if you feel someone is attempting to harm you with hexes or sending bad energy your way.

Cherries: Beloved for their bright red color and taste, cherries are associated with romance and powers of divination. Useful in love spells, the Japanese believe tying a strand of hair from your head onto the blossom of a cherry tree will bring a lover to you.

Figs: Figs hold a place in our culture from the story of Adam and Eve in the Garden of Eden. Unsurprisingly, they are associated with sexuality and fecundity. If eaten ripe off the tree, this fruit will aid in conception and help men with impotence issues. A fig tree grown outside the bedroom will bring deeply restful sleep and prophetic dreams. Outside your kitchen, a fig tree will ensure there will always be plenty of food for your family. Anywhere a fig tree grows will bring luck and safety. A folk charm holds that gifting someone a fig grown by your hand binds them to you. Wield your figs wisely.

Grapes: Planting grapevines grants you abilities for money magic and gardening and farming. The ancient Romans painted pictures of grapes on the garden walls to ensure good harvests and fertility for women. Eat some grapes for mental focus, and magical spell workings for money are abetted greatly by placing a bowl of grapes on the altar.

Lemon: This beloved member of the citrus family confers the rare power of longevity and faithful friendship, purification, love, and luck. The juice from lemons mixed with water can be used to consecrate magical tools and items during the full moon. Dried lemon flowers and peels can also be used in love potions and sachets. Bake a lemon pie for the object of your desire and he or she will remain faithful to you for all time. Imbibing lemon leaf tea stirs lust.

Oranges: Like the joyful color of this fruit, oranges are a fruit of happiness in love and marriage. Dried orange blossoms added to a hot bath make you more beautiful. A spritz of orange juice will add to the potency of any love potion. Orange sachets, pomanders, and other gifts made with this fruit offer the recipient utter felicity; thus, it is an ideal gift for newlyweds.

Peaches: It might seem obvious, but eating peaches encourages love. They also enhance wisdom. An amulet made with the pit can ward off evil. A fallen branch from a peach tree can make an excellent magic wand, while a piece of peach wood carried in your pocket is an excellent talisman for long life.

Pears: It is believed this uniquely shaped fruit brings prosperity and long life. Somewhat similar to peaches, the pear nourishes powers of lust and love. Shared with a partner, pears can be used to induce sexual arousal. Pear wood is also good for magical wands.

Pineapple: While renowned as a symbol of hospitality, pineapples represent neighborliness, abundance, and chastity. Dried pineapple in a sachet added to bath water will bring great luck. The juice hinders lust when consumed. Dried pineapple peel is great in money spells and mixtures.

Plums: Plums are for protection and add sweetness to romantic love. A fallen branch from a plum tree over the door keeps out negative energy and wards off evil.

Pomegranates: Here we have powers of divination, making wishes come true, and engendering wealth. Eating the seeds can increase fruitfulness in childbearing; you can also carry the rind in a pocket sachet. Always make a wish before eating the fruit, for your wish will come true.

Raspberries: This sweet berry has tremendous powers for true love and home safety. Hang the vines at doors when a person in the house has died so that the spirit won't enter the home again. Pregnant women carry the leaves to help with the pains of childbirth and pregnancy. Raspberries are often served at the table to induce love. Raspberry leaves are also carried for luck.

Tomatoes: Reminder: the tomato is a fruit! An easy money spell is to place a fresh-off-the-vine tomato on the mantle every few days to bring prosperity. Eating tomatoes inspires love. They are great to plant in your garden to ward off pests of all kinds.

LOVE IN LIQUID FORM: SPICY CINNAMON LIQUEUR

This popular beverage gives peppy energy and can also be a love potion. These few ingredients can lead to a lifetime of love and devotion:

- 1 cup vodka
- 2 whole cloves
- 1 teaspoon ground coriander seed

- 1 cinnamon stick
- 1 cup simple sugar syrup

Pour the vodka into a large canning jar and add the herbs; cover and place in a cupboard for two weeks. Strain and filter until the result is a clear liquid. Clean the canning jar and dry it thoroughly, then put the clear liquid back in. Add the simple syrup and place it back on the shelf for a week. Store this in a dark-colored bottle that seals; you now have liquid love! You can drink it "neat" on its own or add it to hot chocolate, water, tea, or milk for a delightful drink to share with your loved one.

SWEET AS SUGAR: DIY ELIXIR

You can make simple syrup, a base for any liqueur, in five minutes by boiling a cup of sugar in half a cup of water. The method above can be used to create distinctive after-dinner drinks and digestives from angelica, anise, bergamot, hyssop, all mints, fennel, and, perhaps the most special, violets. To your health!

WAXING MOON: MAGNOLIA LOVE POTION

This spell will ensure a faithful relationship. You will need:

- Magnolia buds gathered under a waxing moon
- Honey

Sweeten the magnolia buds with honey and brew in a tea, sprinkle in a salad, or stir into a soup. Chant this simple spell as you brew or stir:

> *Lover be faithful, lover be true.*
> *Give thy heart to nobody but me.*
> *This is my will.*
> *So mote it be.*

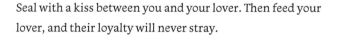

Before you both consume the honeyed magnolia buds, whisper this wish:

> *Honey magnolia, goddess's herb,*
> *Perform this enchantment superb,*
> *Let [lover's name] and I be as one.*
> *With this, the spell is done.*

Seal with a kiss between you and your lover. Then feed your lover, and their loyalty will never stray.

TO YOUR HEALTH!
MULLED MEDIEVAL
MERRIMENT

Start preparing this special mixture by pouring a gallon of unfiltered sweet apple cider into a big pot. Go for organic cider or juice from the farmers' market for the best taste and energetic effects, but it is even better if you can make cider from apples you have gathered or harvested. Take a bottle of your favorite low-cost red wine and gently heat it in a large pot on a low flame. Add sugar, cinnamon, and cloves to your taste, but include at least a teaspoon of cloves and a tablespoon each of sugar and cinnamon. Pour the cider into the warmed wine, and add thirteen whole cloves and six cinnamon sticks. Simmer, stirring every six minutes. Notice how your entire home fills with the spicy sweetness of merriment. After thirty minutes, it will be ready to serve.

CARDAMOM
COFFEE CRUSH

Cardamom is a spice East Indians have used to good effect, as they are the creators of the Kama Sutra. Called the "grains of paradise," you can find it in any grocery store. Organic cardamom can be recognized by the green color of the pods. To get the highly desirable grains, crush the pods in your mortar and pestle and extract the seeds. You will need:

- 1 cinnamon stick
- Cardamom from 6 pods
- ½ cup ground coffee beans
- 6 cups water
- Cream or half & half
- 1 tablespoon honey or raw sugar

Break the cinnamon into pieces and grind together with the cardamom, then stir into the ground coffee. Make coffee as you usually do, whether with a French press or a coffee maker, for four cups brimming with bliss. The strong rich flavor calls for cream and sweetening, so sweeten the pot, then serve it for an amorous and energetic evening.

BELTANE BREW

Honeyed mead is revered as the drink of choice for the sexy pagan holy day of Beltane. It is an aphrodisiac, and with its sticky sweetness, it is perfect for dribbling on your lover's body and then licking it off. This is my special recipe for honeyed mead, handed down through generations of Celtic witches. You will need:

- 1 quart of honey
- 3 quarts of distilled water
- 1 packet of yeast
- Herbs to flavor

Mix the honey and water. Boil for 5 minutes. You can add the herbs in proportions to your liking; I prefer a teaspoon each of clove, nutmeg, cinnamon, and allspice.

Add a packet of yeast and mix. Put in a large container. Cover with plastic wrap and allow it to rise and expand. Store the mixture in a dark place and let it sit for 7 days.

Refrigerate for 3 days while the sediment settles to the bottom. Strain and store in a colored-glass bottle, preferably green, in a cool, dark place. You can drink it now, but it is even tastier after it has been aged for at least 7 months.

Nonalcoholic Mead

- 1 quart honey
- 3 quarts distilled water
- ½ cup lemon juice
- 1 sliced lemon
- 1 half-teaspoon nutmeg
- Pinch of salt

Boil for 5 minutes and then cool and bottle immediately. Keep in the fridge to avoid fermentation, and enjoy.

Chapter Three

RITUAL RECIPES: SWEET TREATS FOR SWEETHEARTS

Saturn-Day Night Fever

It is important to gather your soul tribe and celebrate each other from time to time. Here is a pagan ritual I have performed on weekends—I call it "Saturn-day night fever." Over the years, I have added many embellishments, such as astrological or holiday themes. The basic ritual of cakes and ale, however, is a timeless and powerful classic.

Gather a group of friends either outdoors under the moon or in a room large enough for dancing, drumming, and singing. Have the guest bring a cake and cider, mead, beer, or juice to share. (Note that the cake can be of any style, so it does not have to be an iced sheet cake; banana bread, Irish soda bread, or braided honey bread will do just as well.) Place the offerings in the center of an altar table. Then light a sage leaf and green and brown candles for home and hearth.

Once everyone is seated, the host or designated leader intones:

Gods of nature, bless these cakes,
that we may never suffer hunger.
Goddess of the Harvest, bless this ale,
that we may never go without drink.

The eldest and the youngest of the circle rise and serve the food and drink to everyone in the circle. Last, they serve each other. The ritual leader pronounces the blessing again. Then everyone says together, "Blessed be."

The feasting begins, ideally followed by a lot more ale and lively dancing. A wonderful way to keep a group of friends connected is for a different person to host the circle one Saturday each month.

FOOD OF THE GODS: CHOCOLATE BROWNIES

This is one of the easiest recipes for brownies you will find anywhere. So yummy!

- ½ cup flour
- 1 cup sugar
- ½ cup salted butter, melted
- 2 eggs
- ⅓ cup cocoa powder

Prepare the ingredients. Preheat the oven to 350°F. Grease a 9x9-inch baking pan.

Make the brownie batter: In a medium bowl, combine the flour, sugar, and cocoa powder. In another small bowl, whisk together the butter and eggs. Add the egg mixture into the flour mixture, stirring until just combined.

Bake the brownies for 25 to 35 minutes, or until a toothpick inserted in the center comes out clean. Remove from the oven and let cool for 5 minutes. Cut into 16 squares and serve, perhaps à la mode.

I KNEAD YOU: BRAKING BREAD IS AN ACT OF LOVE

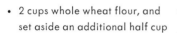

The smell of baking bread is incredibly seductive. Try it, and you'll soon see.

Makes one large or two regular loaves.

Ingredients:

- 2 cups whole wheat flour, and set aside an additional half cup
- 2 cups bread flour
- ¼ cup toasted sesame seeds
- 2 tablespoons active dry yeast
- 2½ teaspoons salt
- 2 cups milk, scalded
- 2 tablespoons peanut butter
- 2 tablespoons honey

First, mix the dry ingredients in a large bowl.

Add the peanut butter and honey to the hot milk and stir to combine.

Cool the milk mixture to warm and pour into the dry ingredients. Knead for 15 minutes, adding the extra flour if needed to make smooth and elastic dough. Oil the surface of the dough, cover with plastic wrap or a damp kitchen towel, and let rise in a warm place until it has doubled in size; this usually takes 90 minutes. Punch it down and shape it into your desired loaf size. Cover and allow to rise again in a warm place.

Bake in a preheated 375°F oven for 30 minutes until golden brown and hollow-sounding when you rap on the bottom. This goes wonderfully with the next few recipes, too.

SOUL-MATE SUPERFOOD SMOOTHIE

A friend came up with this delicious and nutritious smoothie so her beloved husband could get *all the things* in one smoothie. He loves it, and so do we!

- 1 banana
- ½ cup strawberries, sliced

- 4 tablespoons plain yogurt
- 1 tablespoon chlorophyll liquid

- 1 tablespoon hemp oil
- ½ cup orange juice

- 2 tablespoons goji berries, presoaked (optional)
- 1 packet Emergen-C, or vitamin C powder

If you are using goji berries, soak them for 2 hours before you make the smoothie.

Blend ingredients until smooth. Add more orange juice or water if the consistency is too thick for your taste.

Love Crafts: Kitchen Cupboard Incense

As you may have noticed from your reading, I treasure cinnamon incense. It brings positive energy to your space, an appealingly sweet and spicy scent. It also brings prosperity and calm. What could be better? This may become one of your favorites, as it is truly easy to make.

Gather:

- 1 tablespoon ground cinnamon
- 1 teaspoon of water
- Small bowl
- Baking sheet
- Small glass votive container

Spoon the powdered cinnamon into the middle of your bowl and mix the water well. When the consistency is close to that of damp sand, you are good. Using your hands, knead the mixture into your desired shape, a cone, pyramid, ball, or even a heart shape. Place this onto your baking sheet at 325°F for 15 minutes. Pull it out and let it cool. Once your incense creation is room temperature, place it in the glass votive for the hewn you want to use it. These DIY incenses take a few seconds to light, but captivating scents are so worth it.

DIY ENCHANTED INCENSES

- Ginger will bring more money into your space as well as success
- Cardamom is used in love magic and will also bring tranquility
- Allspice is effective in healing work
- **Nutmeg** awakens psyches and prophetic dreams
- Clove is excellent in protection and banishing

GATHERING THE TRIBE
NUT ROAST

Nuts are some of the best food humans can eat; they are packed with positive proteins and beneficial oils and are tasty. This nearly effortless nut roastie is a great snack for movie night at home or party time and makes a savory appetizer for special meals. Here is what you need:

- 10 ounces mixed nuts
- 8 ounces of day-old bread
- 1 medium-sized white onion, chopped
- 1½ cups veggie stock

- Soy or tamari sauce
- 1 teaspoon dried sage
- 2 ounces unsalted butter

Preheat your oven to 350°F and sauté the onion in the butter until softened. Mix the nuts with the bread in a food processor or stir vigorously until blended well, then transfer to a large bowl. Heat the stock to boiling and pour into the mixture in the bowl. Stir in the onions. Season as you see fit with salt, pepper, and sage. Pour in a tablespoon of the soy or tamari sauces to add zing to your roast and give one last stir. Spoon the roastie mix into a greased baking dish and bake for a half hour. Take note as your kitchen fills with a fantastic aroma. Heating the nuts brings out more natural oils and intensifies the flavor. Like herbs and flowers, nuts have magical properties, mainly to increase love and feelings of conviviality and peace, thus the name of this dish. When you serve this roastie, you are quite literally "sharing the love."

GRACEFUL CONNECTION

Before you enjoy this friendly repast together, hold hands and recite this grace:

> *Sister, brother, tribe of the soul, ones who care.*
> *Merry may we meet again to share.*
> *Breaking bread and quaffing mead,*
> *we draw closer in word and deed.*
> *Blessing of love to all!*

BE MY VALENTINE: FOOD MAGIC

Food can set the mood all its own as a prelude to a night of love. Surprise the object of your affection with one of these treats:

- Chocolate is rightly called the "food of the gods."

- Nutmeg is held in high regard as an aphrodisiac by Chinese women.

- Honey—ever wonder why the time after a wedding is the honeymoon? Bee-sweetened drinks are a must!

- **Oysters** have been celebrated since Roman times for their special properties.

- Strawberries lend a sweet erotic taste; eat alongside chocolate for maximum effect.

- Vanilla is little known as an aphrodisiac, but the taste and the scent are powerful.

CHILLED CUCUMBER MINT SOUP IS FOR LOVERS

Cucumber has aphrodisiac qualities, according to recent studies, thanks not just to the veggie's shape but also its scent. This easy-to-grow delight provides several nutrients essential to maintaining sexual health, including manganese and vitamin C, and it is a tonic for vibrant skin. Here is a short and sweet recipe for a refreshingly cold soup to share with a love on a hot day.

- 3 large, peeled cucumbers
- ½ cup fresh mint leaves
- 1 teaspoon kosher salt
- 3 tablespoons olive oil

Put the ingredients in the blender and puree. This gorgeous green potage makes four cups, enough for two servings for a hungry couple. The only accompaniment you need is crispy herb crackers, an icy beverage, and each other.

HOMEMADE SWEET TREAT: CANDIED HERBS

- 1 cup vodka
- 1 cup simple sugar syrup
- 1 cup honey
- 2 cups dried herb of choice
- 1 large sheet waxed paper

One of the byproducts of making herbal honey, liqueurs, and oxymel is candied herbs, which can also be used for snacks and in sweet cakes and cookies. To make a batch, stir the liquids in a big pot and heat slowly, stirring every few minutes. Upon reaching boiling point, add the herbs and stir until well-mixed. Turn down to a slow simmer until the liquid is thick and sticky. Spoon the herbs out and place on wax paper to crystallize. Good herbs for this are hyssop, ginger root, lavender, lemon balm, fennel seed, mint, angelica stems, and thyme, and small slivers of orange, lime, and lemon. The gift of homemade candy is a marvelous way to signal a crush.

HONEYHEART SHORTBREAD

- 1 cup butter
- ⅓ cup honey
- ⅓ cup candied herbs
- 2½ cups flour

Cream the herbs and honey into the softened butter and then fold the flour into it gradually. Mix well and roll into a 2-inch-wide log shape. Wrap this dough in wax paper and chill in the refrigerator at least 2 hours. Preheat the oven to 325°F; slice rounds of the dough and place onto a greased cookie sheet. Bake for 20 minutes or until the top turns golden. Lavender and hyssop make the sweetest dessert shortbreads. Omit the honey from the recipe and use sage and thyme for a highly satisfying breakfast shortbread to serve your sweetheart after an exquisite evening.

LEMON BALM ENCHANTED ICING

You can mend broken hearts and enchant any would-be love interest with lemon balm. This recipe takes the cake, either one of your making or store-bought sponge cake. Try a lemon balm version of the above Sweetheart Shortbread and glaze it with the icing; it will be certain to turn anyone who tastes this into your devotee.

- 6 lemon balm leaves
- 2 tablespoons water
- 8 ounces confectioners' sugar
- 4 drops vanilla extract
- 1 lemon
- 1 candied lemon (using above recipe)

Combine water, vanilla, and lemon balm and soak overnight. Strain out the herbs and add sugar into the liquid. Grate in the zest of the lemon and whisk, squeezing lemon juice if needed for fluid consistency. Pour this icing over the cake and top with sprinkles of candied lemon and lemon balm. This distinctive dessert is a spell spun of sugar.

Chapter Four

SENSUALITY SPELLS AND LUSTFUL ENCHANTMENTS

W itches are so in tune with their sexuality that they have dedicated an entire high holiday—Beltane, or May Day—to sex, as discussed in an earlier chapter. On that day, we celebrate seduction by dancing around the Maypole through the moonlit night and answering our wildest urges with complete abandon. As witches, we appreciate the transcendent nature of sex. After all, we worship the goddess, who embodies the feminine mystique. With her guidance, we revel in the art of lovemaking and taste the full spectrum of erotic pleasure. For centuries, we have honed our craft and developed our mastery of the fiery arts to unleash the power of seduction within us.

Sex resides in a magical realm where body, mind, and soul meet. It is a heightened state where raw emotions and primal passion reach their peak. To make love with another person is to give of yourself completely and receive pleasure with just as much surrender. It is a chance to use every sense, including your intuition, as you blur the lines between your body and your spirit. By practicing Moon Magic, you reach this pure state through the time-tested spells and potions listed in this chapter. As with all witchcraft, turning carnal knowledge into sublime spirituality requires clarity, intention, and authenticity. Conscious sex isn't a random act but the result of focus and self-awareness.

Think of this collection of sex and love spells in this chapter as a sort of "pillow book." It is intended to encourage you and your lover to seek joy and intensity, revel in the heights of ecstasy, and above all, have *meaningful* experiences.

But be forewarned that the sexual power of witchcraft can be scary and threatening to people, so discretion and caution are advised. I urge you to keep your sense of ethics in mind. These sex spells are for positive pleasure between consenting adults. No manipulation, no coercion, harm to none.

Here I have gathered spells of my design along with those passed down from the sisterhood. I have also learned much about sex from the men in my life, and this, too, I share so you can have a juicy and joy-filled sex life. I encourage you to share your secrets, as well. We all have unique gifts and special talents. Pass them on. And please remember, nothing is as sexy as an open mind.

APHRODISIACAL ALTAR: FEEDING THE FIRE OF LOVE

To prepare for new relationships and deepen the expression of feeling and intensity of your lovemaking, you have to create a center from which to renew your erotic spirit: your altar. Here, you can concentrate your energy, clarify your intentions, and make wishes come true. If you already have an altar, incorporate special elements to enhance your sex life. As always, the more you use your altar, the more powerful your spells will be.

Your altar can sit on a low table, a big box, or any flat surface you decorate and dedicate to magic. One friend of mine has her sexy shrine at the head of her bed. Another girlfriend has hers in a cozy closet with a nest-like bed for magical trysts.

Begin by purifying the space with a sage smudge stick, a bundle of sage that you burn as you pass it around the space. Then cover your altar with a large, red, silky-smooth piece of fabric. Place two red candles at the center of your altar, then place a "soulmate crystal" in the far-right corner. "Soulmate" or "twinned" crystals are any crystals that formed fused together. They are available at metaphysical stores.

Anoint your candles with jasmine and neroli oil. Keep the incense you think is the sexiest on your altar as well. For me, it is peach and amber musk, which I simply love to smell. Your sex altar is also a place you can keep sex toys you want to imbue with magic. Place fresh Casablanca lilies in a vase, and change them the minute they begin to fade. Lilies are heralded as exotic *and* erotic flowers prized for their seductive scent.

Sanctify Your Love: Altar Dedication

Here at your magical power source, you can "sanctify your love." Collect your tools, meaningful symbols, and erotic iconography and prepare for the sacred rituals of love.

You'll need:

- Red and pink candles
- Incense
- Victorian violet and rose essential oils

Light the candles and incense and dab the essential oils between your breasts, near your heart. Speak aloud:

I light the flame of desire;
I fan the flame of passion.
Each candle I burn is a wish,
and I come to you as a witch.
My lust will never wane.
I desire, and I will be desired.
Harm to none, so mote it be.

ENTICEMENT ENCHANTMENT: THAT SPECIAL SOMEONE SPELL

This is the perfect spell of enchantment to use when you have met a "special someone" and wish to enhance your charm and magnetism. With this invocation, you are sure to attract your heart's desire. You will need the following supplies:

- 1 red candle
- 1 pink candle

- Essential oil (jasmine and rose have powerful love vibrations to attract and charm a lover)

Stand before your altar with tokens representing love. Light the candles.

Scent your wrists, throat, and left breast over your heart with the same oil.

If you desire sexual results, look into the flame of the red candle. If you desire affection or flirtation, look at the pink candle instead. Said aloud, this spell creates loving energy:

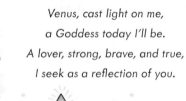

Venus, cast light on me,
a Goddess today I'll be.
A lover, strong, brave, and true,
I seek as a reflection of you.

PENDULUM OF THE RING

This is more of a divination technique to find new love rather than a spell. A big part of meeting someone new is knowing how and when such a meeting may take place. So try a little divination. You need two things: a length of white ribbon or string and a ring. The ring needs to symbolize a wedding ring but doesn't need to be truly valuable.

Tie the ring to the end of the ribbon, and let it dangle from your hand. You need to be very still for this, so you should probably rest your elbow on the table for stability.

Wait for the ring to be still, then ask the pendulum a couple of yes or no questions about your new love and watch the ring. If it starts to move, you can take that as a yes to your question. Use your questions to pinpoint where you will meet this love, not who it will be. After about five questions, thank the ring and put it away for at least twenty-four hours before asking anything else.

GODDESS GLOW RITUAL BATH

Indulge in this sensually satisfying ritual bath that will make your skin glow and surround you with a seductive aura. You will need the following:

- 3 ounces apricot kernel oil
- 3 ounces sweet almond oil
- 1 ounce aloe vera gel
- ½ ounce rosewater
- 13 drops jasmine essential oil
- 6 drops rose essential oil
- 2 ounces dried chamomile flowers and yarrow
- 1 rose or red candle

Shake this mixture in a jar or bottle before pouring into a warm filled tub sprinkled with dried chamomile flowers and yarrow. (If you prefer, you can keep the herbs in the cheesecloth but still partake of their essence by allowing it to infuse into the water.) Light the rose or red candle (for passion), and say:

My heart is open, my spirit soars,
Goddess, bring my love to me. Blessed be.

No towels; air dry afterward.

Enchanted Essential Oils

Essential oils are highly concentrated extracts of flowers, herbs, roots, or resin extract, sometimes diluted in a neutral base oil. Try to ensure you are using natural oils instead of manufactured, chemical-filled perfume oils; the synthetics lack real energy. Also, approach oils with caution, and don't get them in your eyes. Clean cotton gloves are a good idea to keep in your kitchen for handling sensitive materials. You can avoid any mess and protect your magical tools by using oil droppers. While you are learning and studying, find a trusted herbalist or a wise sage at your local metaphysical shop; usually their years of experience offer much useful knowledge you can use to your advantage. I have included as much as I can in this at-a-glance guide to oils. These essential oils are excellent choices for anointing lamps as well as yourself:

- Cinnamon is energetic, spicy, and warm. It stimulates the mind as well as the body.

- Ginger is vigorous and revitalizing and heightens desire and comfort.

- Jasmine sparks sensuality and inspires feelings of positivity, confidence, and pure bliss.

- Lavender is soothing, calming, nurturing, and relaxing.

- Orange is a light, citrusy oil that restores balance and lifts moods, enhancing playful emotions.

- Rose brings youthfulness, enhances self-esteem, aids circulation, and relieves tension.

- Sandalwood is a woody aroma that relieves tension and relaxes tense muscles.

- Ylang-ylang is sweet, floral aroma and used as an aphrodisiac; it is relaxing and reduces worry and anxiety.

BEJEWELED BLESSING: WAXING MOON SPELL

The word "glamour" was originally the word for the ancient art of shifting one's appearance and its effect on the beholder, which over the centuries became linked to the idea of "enhancing one's beauty through artifice." The arts of magic can still be used to accomplish this purpose; bear in mind that the truest beauty comes from within. You can enhance it greatly with this charm. This ritual is best performed during the waxing moon. Gather:

- Vervain, thistle, chamomile, and elderflower
- Salt
- Your favorite jewelry

To prepare for a night of true love, during the waxing moon, take the rings, necklace, and earrings you are planning to wear for an upcoming special tryst and lay them on your altar.

Mix the dried vervain, thistle, chamomile, and elderflower. Cover your jewelry with the herb mixture, and then sprinkle salt on top. Hold the jewelry in your hands and say:

Bless these jewels and the hand and heart of the wearer
with light and heaven above.
May all who look upon me see me through the eyes of love.

SELF-LOVE RITE: BLESS YOUR BODY MEDITATION

When you have made a batch of salts, scrubs, or magic potions for your use or as a gift, stop and count your health blessings with this mindfulness practice. Sit in a comfortable position with your bottle of potions placed in a bowl or dish in front of you. Think about the blessings in your life and the gifts your item offers; visualize your skin and hair gleaming with vitality. Picture your loved ones wearing a big smile as they use your handmade remedies. What are you grateful for at this moment? There is powerful magic in recognizing all that you possess and in having an attitude of gratitude. Breathe steadily and deeply, inhaling and exhaling slowly for twenty minutes. As you meditate, send the positive energy into the bowl containing your personal potion. Now, the blessings are there any time you or a loved one may need them.

SEDUCTIVE SORCERY: MOTHER NATURE'S BEAUTY SECRETS

The best beauty secrets are often hidden among Mother Nature's flora and fauna. Forget spending a fortune on overpriced creams, lotions, masks, and salves; go to your kitchen garden or check your pantry for organic remedies and common beauty solutions. Here are some of the best recipes and natural ingredients to begin a journey toward a healthy and nontoxic beauty regime.

VENUS'S VERY VANILLA SUGAR SCRUB

Sugar scrubs exfoliate the skin while helping it stay nourished with moisture. This recipe could not be simpler, yet it is a delightfully decadent DIY scrub in the tub.

All you need are four simple ingredients:

- ¼ cup brown sugar
- ¼ cup white sugar
- ¼ cup organic olive oil
- 6 to 8 drops vanilla essential oil

Into a small bowl, measure equal parts white sugar and brown sugar. Start with ¼ cup of each type of sugar. Mix sugars thoroughly using a wooden spoon. Now, add the olive oil—the amount used depends on your taste. Use enough oil to coat the sugar well and create a pliable texture. Lastly, add in a few drops of vanilla; I go with at least six drops. You can also try variations on the recipe using all brown sugar and other essential oils. My absolute favorite is equal parts vanilla oil and amber oil, which I call "vamber." It is great to get ready for a date night out on the town. You will look and feel like the goddess of love herself.

PLEASURE OF PARADISE SENSUAL SCRUB

Sandalwood, amber, and vetiver are all rich, earthy scents that combine well together.

- 5 drops sandalwood essential oil
- 5 drops amber essential oil
- 2 drops vetiver essential oil
- ½ cup Epsom salt
- ½ cup baking soda

Combine essential oils with Epsom salt and stir in the baking soda. Mix well; the mixture will become a richly scented paste. You can use it a couple of different ways: one is to slather it onto yourself and shower off with a loofah and thick washcloth. But my favorite way to completely soak up this earthly pleasure is to roll it into a ball after you mix it and place it under the faucet while running a hot bath. The entire room will smell like paradise. Soak it all in; lie back and enjoy this fully.

If you want to store some for the future or give this scrub as a thoughtful gift, you can store it in a lidded plastic one-cup container or roll it into bath bomb balls and let it dry on wax paper or paper towels. This recipe will make three palm-sized bath bombs. Note, you will be asked for more!

LAVENDER LOVE MASSAGE BARS

Massage bars should look, smell, and feel luxurious. Cocoa butter is beloved for its delicious natural chocolate scent. I also recommend shea butter or mango butter as other options, for they are also sumptuous.

- 3 ounces cocoa butter
- 3 ounces beeswax
- 3 ounces almond oil

- 1 teaspoon of lavender essential oil
- Soap bar molds (available at any craft store)

Slowly heat the beeswax, almond oil, and cocoa butter in a double boiler over low heat until just melted. Remove from heat. Add essential oil when mixture has cooled slightly. Pour into soap molds and cool until hardened, approximately 2 hours. Place in the freezer for a few minutes before popping the bars out of the molds. To use, rub massage bar onto the skin— the warmth of the skin immediately melts the bar. Package your handmade massage bars in a pretty basket and give as a thoughtful gift.

GODDESS GUIDE TO DREAMING: PROPHETIC LOVE CHARM

This charm will help you see whether a newfound interest will become long-term. Arrange a romantic evening and prepare this amulet for clairvoyance. Gather these supplies:

- Small red velvet scarf or pouch
- Lavender, thyme, cinnamon, and cloves
- 1 vanilla bean pod
- Jasmine essential oil

Take the velvet scarf or pouch and stuff it with the herbs. Add the vanilla bean pod and a drop of jasmine oil.

Tie the ends together and hold the pouch in both hands until your warmth and energy fully infuse the potpourri. Recite:

Venus, guide my dreams tonight. Is she the one?

Tuck your amulet into a pillowcase before bedtime. On waking, record the night's dream. You will receive your answer immediately.

ROMANCE ROMA STYLE: HEART HERBS

The folklore of the Romani people is replete with love magic, charms, and enchantments. The way to a person's heart can truly be a dish of delight spiced up with magical herbs. Gather:

- Rye
- Pimento

Many Romani women have enjoyed the fruits of long-lasting love by reciting this charm while mixing a pinch of rye and pimento into almost every savory dish. While stirring in these amorous herbs, recite:

Rye of earth, pimento of fire,
eaten surely fuels desire.
Served to he whose love I crave
and his heart I will enslave!

LIGHTING THE LAMP OF LOVE (AND LUST!): ENCHANTED ESSENTIAL OILS

These essential oils are excellent choices for anointing lamps as well as yourself. If you are anointing yourself, you need to use a carrier oil; dilute one part essential oil with three parts carrier oil. I recommend almond oil as it adds to the sensuality without overwhelming the other scents. Before a tryst, take a hot bath and then anoint yourself after you step out of the water. Slather the enchanted essential oil over your entire body and rub it into your skin. You are now ready for a lust-filled evening.

SESAME SENSATION: ENCHANTED BODY OIL

I use this potion as a combination body care oil, massage oil, and lubricant. This is a tip I picked up from a professional who shared her confidential formula with me; she added, "All my clients marvel at how soft and yummy my skin is." I have acquired several trade secrets from her that I have used to great effect. A total goddess, she also has her clients and lovers worship at her sex altar before they make love. I have to note that she has many repeat customers. Gather:

- 1 cup of sesame oil (you can cheat and get the sesame-scented oil from the pharmacy or grocery store, which works just as well in a pinch)

- Clove, cinnamon, and ginger (powdered)

- Bergamot, amber, and jasmine essential oils

- Amber-colored jar

- Magnetite

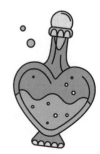

Take the sesame oil and add a pinch of each spice. Then add a drop of citrusy bergamot and a teaspoon of the amber and jasmine oils.

Stir gently and then place in an amber-colored jar with a stopper. Place the jar beside a piece of magnetite, also known as lodestone, which draws people to you. Let it sit for a full week, and then use it to bring yourself and your lover to orgasm—again and again.

Note: This is not for safe sex if using a latex condom. (But there are condoms made from new, oil-friendly materials to be had these days; shop Good Vibrations at goodvibes.com to learn more.)

APHRODISIAC IN A BOTTLE: BLISSFUL BALM

With this blissful combination of oils, you can summon the spirit of love and harmony any day of the year. Amber, rose, and sandalwood essential essences create a sensual scent that lingers on your skin for hours.

- 6 tablespoons almond oil
- 2 tablespoons jojoba oil
- 25 drops sandalwood essential oil
- 3 drops rose essential oil
- 5 drops amber essential oil

Mix oils in a tightly capped brown or dark blue bottle and shake well. You now have an aphrodisiac in a bottle.

Flower and herb-based aromatherapy essences can also be used in diffusers to infuse the air with the desired fragrance. Many of the most sensual essential oils combine well: Try a combination of amber and apple, ylang-ylang and sandalwood, clary sage and rose, or almond and neroli. If you're using a candle diffuser, rose or orange blossom water is an aromatic and romantic alternative to plain water in the diffuser cup.

Additional romantic touches include fresh flowers, which can be used creatively. In Indonesia, lily and orange blossom flowers are scattered on the bed of newlyweds. You can also make a trail of blossoms for your lover to follow; scatter rose petals on your bed or surround your bed with a garland of flowers. Plenty of pillows for lounging, sensuous silk or chenille throws for staying cozy, and your favorite mood-setting music all help cast a spell of romance.

Aphrodisiac essential oils include clary sage, jasmine, neroli, patchouli, rose, sandalwood, vanilla, vetiver, and ylang-ylang.

Witchy Feng Shui for the Romantic in You

Surely one of the main reasons for clearing space in your home and bedroom is to make room for a happy love life. Before you attempt to enhance your prospects of love and sex, you need to create a relationship corner (described in the following pages) and follow these simple steps of "sex shui."

1. Remove all pictures of yourself in which you are alone.

2. Remove all empty cups, jars, vases, and bottles.

3. Remove all photos of past partners or your favorite dead icons (they can go in the hallway).

4. Ensure that there are even numbers of decorative objects such as candles, frames, tables, and so on.

5. Feature special feng shui love symbols such as an open red fan, a pair of dove figurines, or two red hearts; a Victorian or pre-Raphaelite print will work well here, too.

On your bed, use rich, luxurious fabrics and colors; I have a sumptuous burgundy tapestry quilt sewn from handmade Indian saris as my bedspread. It should feel wonderful on the skin and be inviting with comfy pillows, soft silks, and plush velvets.

LUCKY IN LOVE: ASIAN SECRETS FOR OPTIMAL CHI

Your chi is your life's energy, which is of the greatest importance in your home and your bedroom, where you rest and the center of love in your life is located. This feng shui for the bedroom will prevent problems before they even happen! Fill your home with the energy of love and happiness with some of the simplest and most effective magic of all by creating a sacred and safe space for yourself and your loved ones.

Never bring old pillows into a new home. Old pillows can cause poor sleep and bad dreams and can kill a relationship. Old pillows can carry sexual energy, too.

Never place your bed in the center of a room, as it will cause anxiety and get in the way of a healthy sex life.

Never have the foot of the bed facing the door, as it brings bad luck.

Always make the bed and change the linens often to keep your lovemaking fresh.

Place these objects in your bedroom to attract loving energy:

- 2 crystals of rose quartz of equivalent size
- Pink, orange, or red fabric
- 2 red candles

- Images of two butterflies (but never two dead butterflies)

ANOINTING THE TEMPLE OF LOVE: A BED BLESSING

Anoint your bed with this special charm:

- Red cup or gothic goblet
- Jasmine and rose essential oils

In your goblet, mix a half teaspoon of jasmine oil and a half teaspoon of rose oil. Hold it with both hands and speak these words:

> *In this bed, I show my love.*
> *In this bed, I share my body.*
> *In this bed, I give my heart.*
> *In this bed, we are as one.*
> *Here lies my happiness as I give and live in total joy.*
> *Blessed be to me and thee.*

As you say, "Blessed be," flick drops of your bed blessing oil from your fingers across the bed until the cup is empty. Now, lie down and roll around in the bed. After all, that is what it is for!

RING MY BELL: YOUR FENG SHUI RELATIONSHIP CORNER

As you enter your bedroom, the relationship corner will be at the far right in the back right corner. Your love and sex energy will be nurtured there, and you might well consider placing your altar there to serve as your wellspring of Eros.

Look at this area with a fresh eye—what is cluttering your love corner with "dead energy"? Half-empty perfume bottles or near-empty cosmetic bottles could impair your relationship energy. You must cleanse your space of unhappiness and clear the area of clutter by removing all unnecessary objects and tidying up. To further cleanse the area, ring a handbell anywhere clutter has accumulated, giving special attention to your bed linens.

LIGHT MY FIRE: DIY MASSAGE CANDLES

Making massage candles is like making any other type of potted candle. I recommend using soy wax as it is gentle on the skin. Soy is also nice and soft, so it melts easily, stays together in a puddle after melting and can be reused for us thrifty crafters. It won't irritate your skin unless you have a soy allergy; if you have a soy allergy, you can use beeswax instead, which is widely used. (For example, beeswax is in nearly every Burt's Bees product.) The addition of the oils prevents it from hardening again and enables your skin to absorb it. Essential oils or cosmetic-grade fragrance oils are added to create a soothing atmosphere. All soap-making fragrances, also soy candle safe, are perfect choices for scenting your massage candles. Try the basic directions below to make your first candle. For every three ounces of wax, add one ounce of liquid oil and one-quarter ounce of fragrance. I suggest making two candles in four-ounce metal tins while you master this craft.

You will need these elements:

- 2 ounces sweet almond oil or vitamin E oil
- 6 ounces high-quality soy wax
- ½ ounce essential oil
- 2 four-ounce metal tins
- 2 six-inch candle wicks

Melt the soy wax and oil in a double boiler over simmering water. Add the essential oils and stir gently to avoid bubbling or spilling.

Once the wax has cooled somewhat but is still melted enough to pour, place the wicks in your containers and pour the wax. Allow several hours for the candles to set and harden.

Trim the wicks to one-quarter of an inch above the top of the candle, and they're ready to use.

SENSUAL SCENTS FOR MASSAGE CANDLES

Traditionally, these oils have aphrodisiac properties and smell wonderful on your skin and in your home. Just burning the candles will be magical!

Amber, cedarwood, cinnamon, clary sage, jasmine, neroli, patchouli, rose, sandalwood, vanilla, vetiver, and ylang-ylang.

HAPPY AT HOME FIRE RITE

I heartily approve of the Danish tradition of *hygge*, a lovely form of self-care togetherness. The Scandinavians integrate hearth fires into this custom, so we'll take it one step further by adding sacred herbs on top of the wood for a cleansing, purifying, and therapeutic twist to hygge home fires. You can bundle the herbs with string or lay them on top of the unlit wood in your fireplace or outdoor firepot. I do both and speak this spell before lighting the fire:

> *Warmth and love, heart and heat,*
> *Tonight, all good things we shall greet.*
> *These sacred herbs will burn so sweet;*
> *As we gather by this fire and merry meet.*
> *And so it is.*

Now light the fire with your loved one or your lovely self and enjoy the holy smoke.

- Mugwort is an energy cleanser and causes refreshing sleep and meaningful dreams

- Cedar has been relied upon for centuries to clear out the negative. The smell is appealing and widely regarded as a sacred planet in cultures all over the world, where it is used to bless homes

- Sage is beloved for smudging and space clearing, but it is greatly beneficial for meditation and a quiet mind

- **Roses** are sweetness and peace to any space and are also excellent for contemplation

- Sweetgrass, highly prized by Native Americans, brings forth a communal sense and a higher mind

- Bayberry is considered lucky and brings in more pure, positive energies to your home

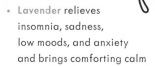

- Lavender relieves insomnia, sadness, low moods, and anxiety and brings comforting calm

- Juniper was long used as a purifying smoke for temples and is now for revitalizing powers

LOOKING FOR NEW LOVE: A NEW MOON CANDLE SPELL

If you are "lookin' for love" and feel like you need the physical release of sex, perform this spell and you will find a lover quickly. This ritual should be performed on the first new moon night for the greatest power. Gather these supplies:

- 2 pieces of rose quartz
- 2 red candles

Take the pieces of rose quartz and place them on the floor in the center of your bedroom. Light both red candles and use this affirming chant twice:

> *Beautiful crystal I hold this night,*
> *flame with love for my delight.*
> *Goddess of Love, I ask of you*
> *guide me in the path that is true.*
> *Harm to none as love comes to me.*
> *This I ask and so it shall be.*

Now, make yourself ready!

BODY BEAUTIFUL RITE: LUST DUST

Nowadays, you can buy body glitter almost anywhere. I've noticed that we witchy types were way ahead on the glitter curve. Whether it is baby powder, body glitter, or the edible Honey Dust sold by the inimitable Kama Sutra body product company, start with a powder that feels comfortable on your body. Get the following supplies:

- Your chosen powder
- 1 drop of amber essential oil
- 1 drop of vanilla essential oil
- 1 teaspoon lotus root powder
- ¼ teaspoon cinnamon (ground)

Add the ingredients to your powder. Stir or shake, then let it dry out before stirring again.

Stand naked and gently rub the powder all over your body while you whisper this charm:

I feel the warmth of your hands.
I feel the hardness of your body against mine.
I feel your tongue.
I am yours for your pleasure.
You are mine for my pleasure.
This dust, our lust,
together, we must!

All day or night, your skin will feel tingly and slightly warm. Notice the interested glances wherever you go. Soon, your body will be a map for exploration.

CELEBRATE YOURSELF: BREAST BLESSING

Celebrate the beauty of your body. Your breasts (and probably all the rest of you) will receive much attention during your lovemaking, so loving attention from you beforehand will consecrate the temple of your body. Get the following supplies:

- 1 cup natural beeswax
- Lemon essential oil
- ¼ cup sesame oil
- Rose essential oil
- Sandalwood essential oil

Take the cup of beeswax, chip it into a double boiler, and heat slowly and gently. Add the sesame oil and stir with a wooden spoon until the wax has melted and blended with the oil.

Let it cool to skin temperature and add:

- 8 drops sandalwood oil
- 2 drops rose oil
- 5 drops lemon oil

Anoint yourself with the oil by dabbing a bit onto your fingertip and then placing it on each nipple, circling clockwise outward until the entire breast is blessed. This should be done slowly, gently, and lovingly as you cup each breast and say aloud:

We all come from the Goddess.
I am she and she is me.
My breasts are holy and wholly beautiful.
I love myself, I love my body, and I love my breasts.
I am consecrated.
Lover, come to me now.

Romancing the Stones: Love Crystals and Gems

Here are stones I recommend for harnessing various powers for love:

- Amber for grounding and understanding yourself
- Amethyst for balance and intuition about other people
- Aventurine for creative visualization so you can picture yourself with a true love
- Bloodstone for abundance and prosperity in your love life
- Calcite for warding off negativity
- Carnelian for opening doors for you and helping you overcome relationship issues
- Chalcedony for power over dark spirits that can get in the way
- Citrine for getting motivated and attracting money and success in all things
- Fluorite for communicating with fairies and other unseen beings
- Garnet for protection from gossip and negative talk
- Geode for getting through periods of extreme difficulty such as breakups or loss
- Hematite for strength and courage and a brave, open heart
- Jade for wisdom to interpret or realize powerful dreams
- Jasper for stability and steadiness in relationships
- Lodestone for bringing a lover back into your life

- Mahogany obsidian for feeling sexy and emanating sensuality
- Moss agate for powers of persuasion and healing
- Quartz crystal for divining your dreams
- Rhodochrosite for staying on course with your life's true purpose
- Rose quartz for love
- Turquoise for safety when traveling and luck in all matters
- Watermelon tourmaline for help with planning your best possible future

DAUGHTER OF VENUS: FRIDAY NIGHT RITE

Venus rules this most popular day of the week. Small wonder that this is the ideal night for a tryst. To prepare for a night of lovemaking, take a goddess bath with the following potion in a special cup or bowl. I call mine the Venus Vial. Perform this rite on a Friday night.

- 1 cup sesame oil
- 6 drops orange blossom oil
- 4 drops gardenia oil
- Bowl

Combine ingredients in the bowl and stir with your finger six times, silently repeating three times:

I am a daughter of Venus; I embody love.
My body is a temple of pleasure, and I am all that is beautiful.
Tonight, I will drink fully from the cup of love.

Pour the Venusian mixture into a steaming bath and meditate on your evening plans. As you rise from your bath, repeat the Venus prayer once more.

Allow your skin to dry naturally. Your lover will compliment the softness of your skin, and indeed, you will be at your sexiest. The rest is up to you.

SPECIAL DATE SPELL: MAKEOUT MAGIC

Ah, the big date you've been looking forward to all week. And you, clever one, planned it on a new moon night. If this new moon happens to be in the signs of Taurus, Scorpio, Libra, or Pisces, you are *really* in for a treat. Here is the last-minute preparation to guarantee you will have the time of your life. Gather the following ritual elements:

- 2 red candles
- Your favorite essential oil (mine is vamber, a concoction of equal parts vanilla and amber oils that makes me feel instantly erotic)

- Thorn of a rose

Take the two red candles and anoint them with your essential oil. Take the thorn and scratch your name on one candle and your lover's name on the other.

Anoint yourself between your breasts and over your heart, and then speak these words aloud twice:

Tonight, under this moon's light,
we will fall under each other's spell.
Tonight, under these stars so bright,
we will ignite a fire and never quell.
With these lips, this mouth, and my art
I will explore the sacred mysteries
of the human heart.

When your object of desire arrives, you should both get comfortable. At an opportune moment, ask your lover to light the two candles. Take their hand and place it over your heart, lean forward, and gently kiss them. For this magic to blossom into full power, you should remain standing and only kiss, slowly and gently but with increasing intensity, for at least thirty minutes. The art of kissing begins with lips only, gently tickling, licking, and nibbling on your partner's lips before moving on to the fabulous French kiss.

PRELUDE TO A KISS: ROMANCE RITUALS

This section of spell work relates to the arts of love, starting with the first kiss. Make that kiss unforgettable! Tattoo your touch onto your lover's skin! Leave more than an impression; most importantly, merge into a oneness that is the truest enchantment. From time immemorial, witches have enchanted everyone with their magical beauty. That's because we know how to supplement Mother Nature's gifts. Before a special evening, I usually employ a "glamour gloss" of my own design so that each kiss is a passion spark. You will need the following:

- Lip gloss
- Oil of clove

Take your favorite pot of lip gloss; add one drop of oil of clove and stir counterclockwise, saying aloud three times:

> *The ripest fruit, the perfect petal,*
> *my lips are as the honey in the flower.*
> *Each kiss a spell of utmost bliss.*
> *So mote it be.*

This will make your lips tingle and give your kisses "spice." The lucky recipient of your kisses will be spellbound.

KAMA SUTRA KISS

The kiss is the gateway to bliss and an amorous experience. The kiss provokes erotic ardor, excites the heart, and is an incitement to the natural gift of yourself that you share with your beloved. After performing the Anointed Lips spell, think of your kiss as an enchantment offering. The following is a list of actual Kama Sutra kisses:

- **Bent kiss:** the classic movie-style kiss where lovers lean into each other

- **Throbbing kiss:** the woman touches her lover's mouth with her lower lip

- **Touching kiss:** the woman touches her lover's lips with her tongue and eyes and places her hands on her lover's hands

- **Turned kiss:** one kisser turns up the face of the other by holding the head and chin and then kissing

- **Pressed kiss:** from below or underneath, one lover presses the lower lip of the other lover, who is above, with both lips

- **Greatly pressed kiss:** taking the lip between two fingers, touching the lip with the tongue, then applying great pressure with the lips upon the lover's lips in the kiss

LIGHTING THE SPARK AND FANNING THE FLAMES

Have you exchanged meaningful eye contact with an appealing stranger at a coffee shop? Seen an artistic-looking individual at a gallery opening? Felt that tug in your tummy, the lingering heat of their gaze? See the following spells for what you can do about it. Simple and powerful love magic ensures you will "merry meet again!"

SUPERNATURAL SOULMATES SPELL

This conjuration utilizes the secret language of flowers to bring your ideal love into your life. With visualization and daily spell work, you can create the love of a lifetime, custom fit to your specifications. Gather:

- 2 candles shaped like human figurines, or two pink candles
- Rosemary essential oil
- Rose essential oil
- 2 fresh roses in your favorite color

Any witchy five and dime will have candles shaped like human figures, usually red in color. Get one each shaped like a man and a woman (or whatever configuration suits your need) and place them on your altar. If you can't find these waxen figures, use two pink candles. Also take the two fresh roses and place them in a vase on your altar.

Rub rosemary essential oil on each candle and do the same with rose oil. Rosemary is for remembrance, and rose is for sweetness and affection. Now light the candles and whisper:

> *Brother mine, brother fair,*
> *new friend of my heart,*
> *merry may we meet and merry may we greet again.*
> *I draw you with my art.*
> *One rose for you; one rose for me.*
> *And so it shall be.*

Each night when you go to sleep, you should visualize your next meeting and what you will say. Each morning, take a moment to meditate on the roses on your altar. Sooner than you think, the mysterious stranger will reappear. Mother Nature, one of the guises of the goddess, will take her course.

Attraction Spell: Two Hearts Beat as One

To transform the object of your desire into your partner in passion, try this powerful attraction spell. Get the following elements for this spell:

- Plain muslin cloth
- Dried sage
- 1 pink seven-day candle
- Red thread and needle or stapler

Take the plain muslin and cut it into two heart shapes. Sew (or staple, if you are in a hurry) the two hearts together, leaving a hole so you can stuff it with dried sage. Then sew it shut and write—or if you are crafty, embroider—the name of the object of your affections onto the muslin heart. Put it on your altar.

Each night at midnight, the witching hour, light the pink candle for thirty minutes beside the heart sachet and say aloud three times:

> *To [crush's name] I offer affection.*
> *To [crush's name] I offer attention.*
> *To [crush's name] I offer joy.*
> *And in return, I shall have the same.*
> *So mote it be.*

Now, your crush will return your attention and be ready to return your affection.

CLEOPATRA'S SECRET

To strengthen the closeness between you and your lover, plan a special evening on the next full moon. It is said this Eastern wisdom mixture may well have been used by Cleopatra when she and Mark Antony made mad love on the banks of the Nile. Gather these on the full moon:

- 1 part amber
- 1 part sandalwood
- 1 part frankincense
- Gardenia oil

Mix the amber, sandalwood, and frankincense, and then add four generous drops of the gardenia oil and grind the mixture together.

You should remove your lover's clothes and walk around them holding the smoking incense bowl to bless their physical body. Then they should remove your clothes and circle you, in your full glory, with the incense.

Now, speak the following full moon blessing together. Or you can do it before your lover arrives, if you prefer, but the spell is more powerful with both of your intentions intertwined.

> *With every word, I draw you closer to me.*
> *With every breath, I do you embrace.*
> *Tonight, we bind our hearts.*
> *Tonight, we twine our bodies.*
> *So mote it be.*

Place the incense beside your bed and sit in a relaxed position facing each other, eyes open. With the lightest possible touch, brush your finger on their skin, starting with the face and working your way down. Go *very slowly*. It should take at least a half hour each for this Tantric Touch spell. Then you should please each other with your hands while looking into each other's eyes. At this point, anything can happen—and should!

BONDS OF LOVE: SEDUCTION SPELL

For heightened and sustained erotic pleasure, try this sacred spell. Gather these elements:

- 2 goblets
- 2 roses, 1 red and 1 white ("fire and ice")
- Nutmeg
- Fine red wine

- 1 yard of red thread
- Red ink and a slip of paper
- Rose essential oil
- Bowl of strawberries

Sprinkle a dash of nutmeg in each goblet. Uncork a bottle of fine red wine for later, allowing it to breathe.

With red ink and a slip of paper, write your lover's name and your hopes and intentions for the night. For example, it could be: "Robert, my gift for you is a full massage and two orgasms." Let your imagination run wild here.

Take the red thread and tie five knots, reciting this as you tie each one:

> *With a knot of one, this spell is begun.*
> *Knot number two, for me and for you.*
> *Knot number three, you come to me.*
> *Knot number four, you knock on my door.*
> *Knot number five, our passion's alive.*

Anoint the red thread with one drop of red wine and one drop of rose oil. Tie the red thread around your waist and place the piece of paper under your bed.

Welcome your lover at the door with the roses, a glass of wine, and a bowl of strawberries, wearing only the red thread. Wear the magic cord until it falls off, usually after thirty days. This is an intense sexual spell, so be prepared to spend a *lot* of time in bed.

NATURE'S OWN STIMULANT: YOHIMBE ROOT RITUAL

Centuries before Viagra, there was yohimbe root, now commonly sold in health food stores. Yohimbe is a potent, natural way to maximize any man's vigor before a special night. Gather the following ingredients for this tea:

- 1 part sandalwood
- 1 part myrrh
- 1 part yohimbe root
- 3 drops tuberose oil

Make an incense by grinding together these ingredients with your mortar and pestle. For the tea, take the root and slice into thin slivers, as you would slice ginger root. When you have at least a half dozen slices, place into a two-cup teapot and pour in two cups of freshly boiled water. Let it steep for five full minutes.

Light the incense and burn it while brewing your yohimbe root tea. Speak the following aloud:

Lover of my heart,

my passion I impart.

Lover of my flesh,

my passion is fresh.

Lover of my mind,

your passion to me binds.

Serve this veritable cup of love to your object of affection and enjoy nature's magic.

HANDS-ON PLEASURE: THE ART OF MYSTICAL MASSAGE

Set the stage for hands-on pleasure before you knead your lover's body into ecstasy. Start with your favorite music. I prefer Indian ragas because they have a naturally sexy rhythm. Whether classical guitar, angelic harps, or an ambient electronic band from Iceland, it should relax and bring pleasure. Light pink, red, and brown candles create a loving, sexual atmosphere that is strongly grounded. Light incense your lover has previously complimented, and lay out towels you have warmed and oils and lubricants you have also warmed. Turn up the heat and turn down the lights to create a "spa" feeling for utter unwinding. I have honey, goose feathers, and an edible raspberry-and-mint rub I like to share as well.

First undress your partner, slowly and gently.

If your partner is open-minded to pagan ways, you should speak this incantation in their presence. If not, it is your silent prayer:

> *I call on you, Pan,*
> *god of the woods, goat, man, and boy.*
> *I ask your blessing on this day of joy.*
> *I call on you, Venus, Goddess of this night,*
> *may we find new seasons of delight.*
> *What I want is here and now.*
> *And so it shall be.*

Start with warmed oil and give a classic massage while your partner relaxes facedown on the bed or massage table. The basic principles of magical massage are rhythmic yet sensitive gliding strokes, gradually shifting to deeper strokes. Use your body weight for firmer pressure.

After relaxing your partner's back, legs, and feet, have them turn over. Massage their chest, arms, and hands. Then glide down to their legs, occasionally brushing the genitals with a light touch. After you finish the legs and feet, slide back up their body and delicately brush the genitals teasingly. Draw the tease out as long as you can so the energy builds and grows. Now is the time to shift the focus to more explicitly erotic activities.

One of the most important tips for an amazing connection: look your partner in the eye as you pleasure them. Locking the eyes and keeping them open during sex will open new dimensions of gratification.

LOVERS' FEASTS: APHRODISIACAL FOODS

Food can be foreplay! Feeding each other can be a wonderful prelude to a night of lovemaking, and of course, a little strategically placed whipped cream and chocolate is a delicious lovers' treat. The following is a list of amazing aphrodisiacs that will ensure pleasure and arousal and help you explore the erotic possibilities of your witch's pantry fully:

- Almonds or erotically shaped marzipan
- Arugula is also called "rocket seed"—need I say more?
- Avocado was referred to by the ancient Aztecs as the "testicle tree"

- Both **bananas** and the flowers of the banana tree have phallic shapes

- Chocolate is quite rightly called "the food of the gods"

- Coffee is stimulating in more than one way

- Figs are another symbol of ultimate femininity—just eating one is a turn-on

- Garlic is the heat to light the flame of desire

- **Honey**—the term **honeymoon** comes from a bee-sweetened cordial, a jug of which was given to newlyweds, the idea being that it would last one full moon (the length of a lunation being four weeks, nearly a month)

- Nutmeg is a traditional aphrodisiac among women in China; eat enough of it and you will hallucinate

- Oysters were prized by Romans for their effect and resemblance to a woman's genitals

- Strawberries—well, why do you think erotic literature so often compares them to nipples?

- Vanilla is captivating for both the scent and flavor

- **Wine** drunk from each other's mouths is unspeakably erotic

RED HEART RUBIES RITE

If you are like me, you can't exactly afford to buy a ruby on impulse. But I have been gladdened lately by the appearance of three-dollar "rough rubies" at a shop at Haight and Ashbury in San Francisco. If you don't have a store like that near you, you can shop online at www.ScarletSage.com, as they have wonderful stones from around the world. Rubies are stones of

great passion. Here is a simple way to light a flame by day that
will catch fire with your lover by night.

Hold your ruby in your left hand over your heart and speak
these words aloud three times:

> I can feel the heat of your skin
> and your mouth.
> I can taste the kisses sweet.
> Your hands on me;
> my hands on you.
> Oh, lover, hear my song.
> Tonight, we will be as one,
> all night long.

Now carry your heart-warmed red ruby in your pocket all day.
Don't forget to give your lover a call and invite them over for a
long and lovely night.

ᴇʟɪxɪʀ ᴏf ᴇᴄsᴛᴀsʏ:
ᴅɪʏ ᴄʀʏsᴛᴀʟ ᴍᴀɢɪᴄ

Elixirs are simple potions made by placing a crystal or gemstone
in a glass of water for at least seven hours. Remove the stone
and drink the "crystallized" water. The water will now carry the
stone's vibrational energy, the essence of the crystal. This is one
of the easiest ways to take in crystal healing, and it is
immediate. The red stones always hold the "lust for life," so to

push the envelope, put as many red stones into your elixir as you can get your hands on. Gather the following:

- Red stones and crystals such as carnelian, garnet, rough ruby, red coral, red jade, red jasper, red sardonyx, cuprite, aventurine, or red calcite
- Jar or glass full of water
- Amber incense
- Red candle

Mix and match the red stones, and remember, if you only have access to one rough ruby and a tiny chunk of red jasper, so be it—that is still a lot of love in a jar.

Add the stones and/or crystals to the jar of water. Place the Ecstatic Elixir in the love corner of your room or on your altar. Light the amber incense and red candle and say aloud:

This jade is my joy, this garnet my grace.

Leave the water on your altar for seven hours or overnight, and drink it upon awakening. Your life energy will quicken, and you should feel upbeat and "good to go."

Chapter Five

LOVE BY THE STARS, SUN, AND MOON

Star-Connected Friends

I rely upon my knowledge of astrology to inform me whether a new acquaintance has the potential to become a dear friend. While the elements are a major indicator of compatibility, you should endeavor to have your astrological charts done and compare them. Finding the sun and the moon in the same sign is common among many soulmates.

Fire Signs:
Leo, Sagittarius, and Aries

People with these signs are bold, courageous, and fun-loving, and they play well together.

WATER SIGNS:
Cancer, Scorpio, and Pisces

These mysterious folks are sensitive, passionate, and creative, and they comfortably swim in the same current.

Air Signs:
Gemini, Libra, and Aquarius

These smart, talkative, and artistic people speak the same language.

EARTH SIGNS:
Taurus, Virgo, and Capricorn

These practical, savvy, and successful types enjoy helping each other to the top.

If you are born on one of the "cusp" days, consider it a blessing. You get along with everybody!

SYNASTRY: ZODIAC SECRETS OF COMPATIBILITY

The specialized astrology of relationships is called "synastry"; it is endlessly fascinating and well worth anyone's study. Liz Greene's brilliant book *Astrology for Lovers* is the best on the subject, and you will turn to it again and again. By learning the sun and moon signs of your love interest and comparing them to yours, you can determine your compatibility in every regard. With Dark Moon witches, who are even more romantic and sensitive than mundanes, it is even more important to keep track of the moon. A basic knowledge of synastry, the sexy side of the stars, can take you far!

The best relationships happen when one person's moon sign is the same as the other's moon. Opposites also attract, as many a lusty Leo and quirky Aquarian can attest, so you should also check out the person right across from you in the zodiac. Some of the most delightful and exciting sex happens when people are different and complement each other with refreshing new sex techniques. This section will provide you with the basics.

FIRE LOVERS

Fire signs are intense, usually positive, and often impetuous. Fire signs get things moving. They are passionate and need a matching enthusiasm in the bedroom in their partner. Fire signs belong together. Sparks can also fly if your moon or Venus is in a fire sign.

Warrior Aries angers easily, but the "kiss and make-up" part can be fun. Tell a Leo he or she is wonderful and sexy (and she or he really is), and you will be amply rewarded with dramatic fireworks between the sheets. Adventurous Sagittarians like to make love outdoors. Try a hike followed by skinny-dipping and an erotic workout.

Air Lovers

Air signs are the great communicators and philosophers/ techies of the zodiac. They are always thinking. These fun and social creatures get along with everyone, although earth signs may try to keep them too grounded. They live in a world of ideas and can at times intellectualize sex. You can turn this trio on with sex toys, porn, and books of erotica. Geminis are verbal during sex, so a little erotic talk can drive them crazy with desire. Libras are the most partnership-oriented of all signs, so a romantic approach is likely to work extremely well with them. Libras are ruled by Venus and have refined lovemaking into an art form. Aquarians are wildly experimental. Together, you'll go through all the Kama Sutra positions and beyond.

EARTH LOVERS

Earth signs are at once solid, practical, and extremely sensual. Grounded and security-oriented, they are the most involved with the physical body of anyone in the zodiac.

Taureans are ruled by Venus, so they are amorous. Bring a fine wine and food into the bedroom for an after-sex snack. Soft fabric, good music, perfumed oils—all senses are explored with Taurus bulls in bed. Virgos are not stereotypical fussy neatniks. They are highly skilled and service-oriented lovers—two wonderful attributes, erotically speaking. Capricorns work just as hard in the bedroom as they do in the boardroom. Support them as they strive for success, and you will be amply rewarded by an attentive lover who will sweep you off for weekend trysts.

WATER LOVERS

Water is the most emotional and sensitive of the signs. Water signs feel things intensely, and their empathy and sensitivity can make for exquisite sex—a passionate group. Cancers are nurturing; this is a lover who will take care of you and meet your every need, sexual and otherwise. They are home-oriented, so the bedroom should be a place with every comfort and erotic toy. Scorpios are reputedly the most passionate of *any* sign—they are walking sex, and they know it. They love mystery and want to make love for hours. In bed and out, they want to dominate and own you. Whisper that you want that, too, at the exact right moment for ultimate pleasure. Pisceans are dream lovers, so intuitive they can anticipate your every need and give you unceasing sensuous attention. These trysting fish would *never* get out of bed if they didn't have to.

—

Once you are grounded in a good understanding of your sign and astrological chart and those of your friends and significant others, you can use this new knowledge to enhance your life and well-being and bring joy to the lives of others. Astrology is an excellent tool to help you understand yourself and others. It is also a science handed down through the centuries. Each sign and planet have many associations and magical correspondences. By learning about these correspondences, you can wisely wield the art of astrology.

ASTROLOGY'S HISTORY

The ancient art and science of astrology comes down to us from six thousand years ago, when the Sumerians, denizens of the "cradle of civilization" in Mesopotamia, began marking the metaphysical meanings of the map of the stars. Their neighbors in Ur, the Chaldeans, took this knowledge a step further when they observed certain affinities between precious gems and "star seasons." At the time, their interests were primarily abundant crops, bounteous babies, and less plentiful enemies. But the canny Chaldeans were great record keepers, and they noticed that these recurring patterns tracked with the sky chart and that constellations helped them predict what would happen at certain times of the year. Their greatest minds, scholar-scientists and mathematician-philosophers, cocreated what would become the dense and deeply meaningful pursuit of astrology. Once they got going, they could predict the future, as evidenced by the great biblical story of Jesus' birth and the three kings—astrologers all.

Six thousand years ago, learned men were often also priests, doctors, and seers, along with astronomers and teachers. These special groups of men were also the gemologists who cut, polished, and studied the gems, rocks, and crystals of their earthly domain. They knew which gems should accompany the dead to the underworld, which rocks portended good fortune when hung over doorways, and which crystals offered benefits to the body.

The ancient Sumerians had enormous knowledge, for example, about the Dog Star, properly referred to as Sirius A, and its mate, Sirius B. They knew the densities of the stars and the duration of

their orbit (fifty years), and since Sirius A was the brightest star in the night sky, they connected it to the beautiful blue stone they considered to be powerful and precious: lapis lazuli. They devised a color-coding as the basis for their system.

- Rose and red for planet Mars
- Green for Venus
- **Blue** for Mercury
- Yellow for the sun
- Purple for Saturn
- Light blue for Jupiter
- White for the moon

This was the basic beginning point for a study that would grow and continue for thousands of years, but it was the basis for today's chemistry and astronomy and the human study of astrology. Without knowing about the big bang theory, the Chaldeans and Sumerians still knew we are all made of the same stuff and come from the same place. We are all interconnected; the minerals from the meteorites that fall from the heavens are of the same minerals and elements as our terrestrial rocks. The spectacular creation process, stemming from the original biggest of bangs, is still happening. Diamonds result from millions of years and pounds of pressure on coal, a rather unlovely hunk of earth. The diamonds on our ring fingers started as coal under our feet.

The universe revolves around us in regular cycles, and change happens at every moment. So, like the clever Chaldeans and the scholarly Sumerians, let us see what we can learn from the stars in the sky and the rocks beneath our feet. Let us learn from patterns, cycles, and connections between the earth and sky.

SIGN BY SIGN

We started as sun worshippers on this planet, and the sun is the center of our planetary system, as my birthday mate (February 19) Nicolaus Copernicus pointed out long ago. Composed mostly of hydrogen and helium, our fantastic and fiery sun is a midsized and rather ordinary star in the whole scheme of things. An impressive 870,331 miles in diameter, the sun is 300,000 times the size of the earth, and it affects all bodies within a range of nearly a billion miles, which is why Earth and all the other planets circle it so loyally. The temperature at the sun's core has been estimated at seventeen million degrees Centigrade, with a surface heat of 5,500 degrees. Astrologically, the sun is linked with the sign of Leo, the Lion. Naturally, fire is the element of our sun. Around "Old Sol" all the planets rotate, pulled by the star's gravitational force. Each of the stones and astrological signs has an associated planetary influence.

Each sign also has a precious gem: a talismanic power stone. Talismans are lucky tokens, and I highly recommend them

as altar crystals. Use these rocks and gems to augment your
magical workings and wear them for healing and protection.

Aries: First Half

| March 20 to April 3 | Lucky Golden Charm: Sunstone |

Sunstone, ruled by Mars, is the talismanic stone for early Aries
folks. Appropriately red with an incandescent glow, sunstone
is a gold-flecked good luck charm. Jasper and heliotrope,
commonly called bloodstone, are the other talismans for this
part of the year. Jasper is an opaque and fine-grained variety of
chalcedony. It is found in all colors, including
red, brown, pink, yellow, green, gray/white,
and shades of blue and purple. Bloodstone
is a green stone with red spots. It also occurs
in shades of dark green with red, brown, and
multicolored spots. Iron-laden minerals cause deep
red and brown colors.

Aries: Second Half

| April 4 to April 18 | Maori Treasure: Bowenite |

The talisman for this half of Aries is bowenite, a mossy green-
colored stone of great strength and power. While many of the
crystals designated for late Aries are red or pink, the green
bowenite signifies the other side of the planet Mars. Bowenite

is especially precious and sacred to the Maoris of New Zealand, where some of the finest specimens of this mineral come from, and to the ancient Indians and Persians.

Taurus: First Half

April 19 to May 2	Marbled Miracle Malachite

The talisman for the first half of Taurus is another gorgeous green stone: malachite, corresponding again to the planet Venus. An earthy rock, it is befitting to this earth sign of the zodiac and has many magical tales to its credit. Malachite is said to help regenerate body cells, create calm and peace, and aid one's sleep.

A stunningly gorgeous stone, malachite is worn by many to detect impending danger by using it for scrying. This beautiful green stone offers bands of varying hues and is believed by many to lend extra energy. It is believed that gazing at malachite or holding it relaxes the nervous system and calms stormy emotions. Malachite is said to bring harmony into one's life. It is also believed that malachite gives knowledge and patience.

TAURUS: SECOND HALF

May 3 to May 19	Jadeite for Luck

Jadeite, the lucky stone for later Taureans, comes in many colors. Jadeite also rings with a lovely tone when struck, and this is the most naturally musical sign. This stone calms the soul and heals the bones. Jadeite also abets the easy expression of love, enabling you to say what is in your heart honestly and easily.

GEMINI: FIRST HALF

May 20 to June 4	Mercurial Moss Agate

Moss agate, a form of quartz with a plant-like pattern caused by metallic crystalline grains, perfectly represents the dualism of the twin-signed Geminis. The ancients believed it was fossilized moss inside the stone with dark green markings inside and often used it for water divination. Moss agate is associated with the metal-rich planet Mercury, ruler of the sign of the twins. This stone makes a great grounding stone for this airy air sign; Geminis need to keep their feet on the ground, making this member of the quartz family the perfect talisman stone for this sign.

Gemini: Second Half

June 5 to June 20	Twin Geodes

Geodes, which usually come in two split halves, are the ideal soul stone for late Geminis. Geminis must be *both* halves. This will help integrate the two parts of their nature and make for a complete and whole person. Geodes are formed from old volcanic bubbles and are usually solid agate outside with a center of gorgeous amethyst, opal, or rock crystal. I recommend keeping one of the geode halves at home on your altar or in a special spot where you can see it every day. Keep the other half at your place of work, reflecting and connecting the two parts of the Gemini nature.

Cancer: First Half

June 21 to July 4	Pearls: Lunar-Ruled Gems

Pearl is the talisman of early Cancer natives. Pearls have a long and rich history, first written about in China four thousand years ago and celebrated in all the ancient cultures of the world since humankind first opened a shell and found the prize inside. As Cancerians are the great historians of the zodiac with their incredible memories, pearls are connected to Cancers through the ocean and the tides since their ruler, the moon, influences the flow of the earth's waters. Cancers should wear pearls occasionally, not constantly, and are well advised to decorate their homes and workspaces with shells to honor their native water element and stay secure, refreshed, and relaxed. This will enable Cancerians to avoid their great nemesis: worry.

CANCER: SECOND HALF

July 5 to July 21	Red Coral for Vitality

Red coral is the talisman for the second half of Cancer. Coral is composed of stone formed by lime secreted by sea creatures. One memorable old story associated with oceanic coral is the ancient Greek belief that sea sprites stole Medusa's severed head and took it to the ocean bottom and that each drop of her blood formed a red coral. It was (and still is) believed to have healing and protective qualities. For Cancers, red coral is good for vitality, and a symbol of life, love, and health.

LEO: FIRST HALF

July 22 to August 5	Zircon Bright as Stars

Early Leos can count zircon as their talisman, a stone beloved by early cultures. They resemble diamonds in many ways, except for their chemical compounds and the simple fact that they are not as rare or hard as diamonds. There is much lore throughout history regarding the brilliant zircon; it was believed to be a safeguard against poison and thought to be a holy healer in ancient India. In the early Roman Catholic Church, it was held to be a sign of humility. For Leos, whose downfall can be pride, zircon can guard against this and keep astrological Lions on an even keel.

LEO: SECOND HALF

August 6 to August 21	Solar Stone Heliodor

Heliodor, named for the sun, is the ultimate talismanic stone for late Leos. Heliodor is a member of the beryl family, the sunny yellow sister stone to the emerald (green beryl) and aquamarine (blue beryl). Heliodor is formed under high temperature and pressure. Heliodor can help Leos call on their greatest qualities and talents and provide the impetus for Leos to try to make their dreams come true.

VIRGO: FIRST HALF

August 22 to September 5	Labradorite Unlocks Talent

The early Virgos' talisman is labradorite, the lovely iridescent stone originally discovered in Labrador. Virgos are also ruled by Mercury, as are Geminis, and this quicksilver, peacock-hued crystal is good for mental swiftness. Virgos constantly feel the need to accomplish all their goals for this life. This type of feldspar can reflect every color of the spectrum and helps keep Virgos from becoming too task-oriented or focused on one thing. No one can work harder than a Virgo, and a labradorite can prevent exhaustion from overwork and ensure that early Virgos can activate other talents.

Vɪʀɢᴏ: Sᴇᴄᴏɴᴅ Hᴀʟғ

September 6 to September 22	Visionary Stone: Tiger's Eye

Tiger's eye, another iridescent stone, is the late Virgo talisman; it has qualities of strength, courage, and great perception. Virgos are the great critics, missing no flaws, and tiger's eye can help them to also have great vision and see wonderful possibilities. Tiger's eye typically has lustrous alternating brown and yellow bands, and to some, this resembles the eye of a tiger, hence the name. Tiger's eye is used for focusing the mind. It is said that tiger's eye offers protection during travel and strengthens convictions and confidence. This warm stone benefits the weak and sick as a protective talisman.

LIBRA: FIRST HALF

| September 23 to October 6 | Gorgeous in Green: Dioptase |

Dioptase is the talisman for early Libras. A deeper green than any emerald, dioptase has an extensive copper content. Venus is associated with green, and the intensity of this gorgeous green stone makes it a love crystal for Libras in relationships and higher love for humankind. Dioptase can awaken the spiritual side of Libras, making this usually attractive sign even more beautiful inside and out. Dioptase is difficult to cut for jewelry because of its brittleness, but it can be placed in its crystal form and is also a lovely object to place in uncut crystal clusters all around the home, in shrines, and the bedroom.

LIBRA: SECOND HALF

| October 7 to October 22 | Imperial Stone: Jade |

Like Taurus, the late Libran's talisman is green jadeite, sometimes called "Imperial Green Jade." The Chinese, who have highly prized the stone they call "Yu Shih" in their lengthy history and culture, believed that this type of jade contains all that you need for a long, happy life: courage, modesty, charity, wisdom, and most important for the Libra scale to be in balance, justice.

Scorpio: First Half

October 23 to November 6	Rarest of Blue Stones

Early Scorpios have a most unusual talisman stone: Blue John, found in only one place in the world, in the underground caverns beneath a hill in the county of Derbyshire, England. Blue John is the rarest of fluorites, with dark blue and reddish-purple bands on a white background, and it is related to Pluto, the second ruling planet of Scorpio. Scorpio is the sign of the underworld and secrets, and the origin of the name of the early Scorpio talisman is a mystery no one has yet solved. While Blue John is difficult to come by, other fluorites are more common, and a blue fluorite will substitute nicely for Blue John. Fluorite is a stone that heals bones and wounds beneath the surface, such as broken blood vessels or infections. Secretive Scorpios carry many hurts beneath their strong exteriors, and over time fluorite can gently resolve them.

SCORPIO: SECOND HALF

| November 7 to November 21 | Purple Power: Amethyst |

Everybody thinks of amethyst as the February crystal for
Aquarians and Pisceans, but it is also the talisman for late
Scorpios. The purple color relates to the purple dwarf planet
Pluto and is a stone corresponding to the element of water.
Scorpios are the third water sign, and amethyst can open
the love vibration for Scorpios. Wearing amethyst jewelry
and keeping chunks of amethyst crystal in the home and the
workplace can reveal the sweet, funny, smart, approachable,
and loveable side of a Scorpio, thereby offering a much greater
chance for happiness for this most misunderstood and
enormously powerful sign.

SAGITTARIUS: FIRST HALF

| November 22 to December 5 | Organic Crystal: Amber |

Amber is the talisman for early Sagittarians; this rock formed
from fossilized tree sap and resin is an organic crystal. Amber
was thought by the ancients to have trapped the sun,
and it was called "electron" by the Greeks,
who observed its negative electrical charge.
Amber keeps your energy surging, which
is good for wildly active Sagittarians,
but it can be weakening if worn all the

time, as even Sagittarians can become exhausted. Amber helps performers—actors and musicians swear by it.

SAGITTARIUS: SECOND HALF

December 6 to December 20	Eye of Ra: Turquoise

Late Sagittarians have a turquoise talisman. This rock has a rich and colorful history, and it was prized in the extreme by Persians, Egyptians, Mexicans, Bedouins, Chinese, Tibetans, Native Americans, and Turks. Sagittarians are the centaurs of the zodiac, half-man, half-horse, and turquoise is therefore a strong fit as it is associated with horses and riders. Turquoise, once revered as the "Eye of Ra," lends great sight and aids travel. Wearing this stone will help people born in this part of the year to find their purpose, harness their passion, and maintain the vision to see it through.

CAPRICORN: FIRST HALF

December 21 to January 6	Steadfast Stones

Early Capricorns have jet and lazulite as their talismans, both of which are stones with a dark and shadowy appearance representative of the Capricornian planet of Saturn. Jet, named for its intense black color and hardness, is one of the oldest stones known to man, making it a perfect match for slow and steady Capricorns, who are reputed to grow more youthful as they get older. Capricorns have great longevity; they live long and prosper! Lazulite, opaque and often displaying the dark and cloudy blue associated with the energy of the planet Saturn, is good for mental processes and stimulates the frontal lobe. Dogged and hardworking Capricorns will do well to always keep this concentration-enhancing talisman nearby.

CAPRICORN: SECOND HALF

January 7 to January 19	Saturn Blue Lapis

Late Capricorns get to have lapis lazuli as their talismanic crystal. This stone was revered by the Egyptians and other Mesopotamian cultures. With its bright saturnine blue, this stone connotes wisdom, accomplishment, and value, as befits the latter half of Capricorn. Capricorns sometimes seem slow and plodding to others, but they are anything but. Capricorns are surefooted and careful and will get to the top of the mountain while others fall behind.

AQUARIUS: FIRST HALF

January 20 to February 3	Otherworldly Onyx

Onyx is the deep, dark talisman for early Aquarians: a stone beloved by the people of prehistory and craftsmen of the classical era. It was one of the first stones to be used both as a tool and for decoration by the ancients. Another option for early Aquarians is moldavite. With its otherworldly meteoric origins, it is perfect for the Uranian "bolt from the blue" these scientist-philosophers represent. Moldavite is a mysterious and powerful crystal with many mist-shrouded legends and theories connected to it. No doubt an Aquarius will get to the bottom of it all one day. Visionary Aquarians are some of the greatest thinkers and scientific researchers of the entire zodiac, and they frequently awe us with their discoveries.

Aquarius: Second Half

February 4 to February 18	Earth Star Stone: Diopside

Diopside is the beautiful blue talismanic gemstone for the late Aquarians. This stone corresponds to Uranus, the official ruling planet of Aquarians, and Saturn, their former ruler before Uranus was discovered. In the same way, the gem-grade mineral diopside was discovered comparatively recently. In 1964, star diopside, an included type, was found; it is a magical and stunningly gorgeous stone with a starstruck quality of electric enlightenment, like these February-born inventors, artists, and creative types. Diopside is believed to improve intellectual, mathematical, and analytical abilities, bringing practicality to these applications. This is the perfect talismanic stone to bring airy Aquarians back to Earth.

PISCES: FIRST HALF

February 19 to March 4	Triple Moon Stones

Interestingly, the sign of the fish is affected by three moons attached to three planets: Triton, Io, and our moon. The gem for this sector of the astrological wheel is the oceanic blue-green diamond, which corresponds to Neptune, the ruling planet of Pisces. Aquamarine also relates to all three of the aforementioned moons and is a second talisman for the fish, a dual sign that needs dual crystals. Aquamarine was once believed to be the dried tears of sea nymphs.

PISCES: SECOND HALF

March 5 to March 19	Stone of Spirit: Chrysoprase

The talismanic stone for the late Pisces people is the apple-green type of chalcedony known as chrysoprase. This is a stone that has been revered through the ages. Chrysoprase was associated with sovereignty and utilized by high priests of nearly every era. This crystal is perfect for the sign that can attain the highest level of spiritual evolution. Crystal lore says that chrysoprase bridges the awareness of the spiritual self and physical self. This brings healing, joy, and laughter. It is said that chrysoprase teaches how to love life and yourself—and your shortcomings.

PLANT WISDOM FOR YOUR SPELLS: ASTROLOGICAL HERBOLOGY

You can choose the herbs for your shrine or love altar based on your sun or moon sign. You should explore using celestial correspondences when making tinctures, incense, oils, potpourri, and other magic potions for your rituals. For example, if the new moon is in Aries when performing an attraction ritual, try using peppermint or fennel, two herbs sacred to the sign of the ram. Or if you are creating a special altar for the time when the sun is in the sign of Cancer, the crab, use incense, oils, teas, and herbs corresponding to that astrological energy, such as jasmine and lemon. The correspondences create a synthesis of energies, adding to the effectiveness of your ceremonial work.

- Aries, ruled by Mars: carnation, cedar, clove, cumin, fennel, juniper, peppermint, pine

- Taurus, ruled by Venus: apple, daisy, lilac, magnolia, oak moss, orchid, plumeria, rose, thyme, tonka bean, vanilla, violet

- Gemini, ruled by Mercury: almond, bergamot, mint, clover, dill, lavender, lily, parsley

- **Cancer**, ruled by the moon: eucalyptus, gardenia, jasmine, lemon, lotus, rose, myrrh, sandalwood

- Leo, ruled by the sun: acacia, cinnamon, heliotrope, nutmeg, orange, rosemary

- Virgo, ruled by Mercury: almond, bergamot, mint, cypress, mace, moss, patchouli

- Libra, ruled by Venus: catnip, marjoram, spearmint, sweet pea, thyme, vanilla

- Scorpio, ruled by Pluto: allspice, basil, cumin, galangal, ginger

- **Sagittarius**, ruled by Jupiter: anise, cedar wood, sassafras, star anise, honeysuckle

- Aquarius, ruled by Uranus: gum acacia, almond, citron, cypress, lavender, mimosa, peppermint, pine

- Pisces, ruled by Neptune: anise, catnip, clove, gardenia, lemon, orris, sarsaparilla, sweet pea

- Capricorn, ruled by Saturn: mimosa, vervain, vetiver

CHAPTER SIX

MAGIC MINERALS: CRYSTAL CHARMS AND ROMANCE ROCKS

ROCKS FOR ROMANCE

AMBER—EMOTIONAL HEALING POWER

The Norse believed it to be Freya's tears that fell into the sea when she wandered the earth weeping and looking for her husband, Odin. Her tears that fell on dry land turned into golden amber. For this reason, amber is believed to be helpful and comforting to those who are separated and/or getting divorced, especially women and those experiencing grief.

DIAMONDS—SHARDS OF THE STARS

Diamond has become a symbol of fidelity and is the traditional stone used in a ring for engagement, a pledge to be married and together forever. Since this gem is an aid to intuition, the ring will help the potential bride know if her betrothed is "the one." Diamonds also imbue courage and can help one face anything.

EMERALDS—HEART STONES

Emerald is truly a heart stone, offering benefits on physical and emotional planes. I prefer emeralds above all other stones for engagement rings. This is your ultimate gem for happiness in a relationship. In fact, emerald has been called the stone of successful love and can engender utter felicity, total loyalty, and domestic bliss in a willing couple. The emerald is at its most powerful if worn as a pinkie—or ring—finger ornament or in a bracelet on the right wrist. But wearers, be warned: Do *not* wear emerald at all times, or its super-positive force starts to reverse. A little emerald luck goes a long way.

GARNETS—THE COLOR OF LOVE

Red garnets are love stones. These sexy stones can help those with a lethargic libido tune into their passion. Green garnets are the real emotional healing stones. These crystals offer protection to the chakras. You should wear green garnets as earrings or a necklace to get the most benefit from the inner and outer healing power.

JADE STONE—JUST FOR LOVE

Jade brings with it the power of love and protection. It is also a dream stone, promoting prophetic and deeply meaningful dreams.

- Purple jade heals a broken heart, allowing understanding and acceptance in and pain and anger out. If you are going through a breakup, purple jade will help you with the heartache.

- Green jade is the counselor stone and can help troubled relationships become functional instead of dysfunctional; this shade is also a boon for the brain. Green jade helps with getting along.

- Red jade promotes the proper release of anger and generates sexual passion. Serve your lover a passion potion in a cup of carved red jade while wearing only red jade. Sparks will fly!

- **Blue jade** is a rock for patience, composure, and conveying a sense of control. Wear blue jade pendants for serenity.

- Yellow jade is for energy, simple joy, and maintaining a sense of being a part of a greater whole. A yellow jade bracelet or ring will help you feel all is well in your world.

Jasper—A Jolt of Love Energy

Red jasper can bring emotions that lie beneath the surface to the forefront for healing. This stone is connected strongly to the root chakra, the source of sexual energy and kundalini. If you would like to explore the sacred sexual practice of tantra, both partners could wear red jasper, the stone of passion. Red jasper can be a tool for rebirth and finding justice.

Malachite—Heart Magic

Malachite opens the heart and throat chakras and rebalances the solar plexus, enabling the realignment of the psychic and etheric bodies. Malachite is best used as a ring on your right hand.

Moonstone—Lucky in Love

Moonstone opens the heart chakra and, importantly, helps overcome any anger or hard emotions toward the self. Certain cultures have seen this as a Goddess crystal for millennia and see it as a source of nurturing, wisdom, and intuition. Moonstone is a powerfully protective and loving talisman for pregnant women. In India, moonstone is sacred and lucky but is even more valued in the subcontinent because it helps make you more spiritual. Moonstone is at its best on your behalf if worn in a ring with a silver setting.

Relationship Rescue

If you and your mate are not getting along of late, turn to this romantic remedy rock: moonstone. Moonstone can reunite loved ones who have parted in anger. This lovely, shimmering stone also imparts luck in love. Keep moonstone around, by all means!

OPAL—CUPID'S STONE

In the classical era, humans believed that opals were pieces of rainbows that had fallen to the ground. They also dubbed this exquisite iridescent gem Cupid's stone because they felt it looked like the love god's skin. The Arabs believed opals fell from heaven in bright flashes of lightning, thus gaining their amazing fire and color play. The Romans saw opals as symbols of purity and optimism. They believed this stone could protect people from diseases. The Roman name for opal is so beautiful and evocative— *cupid paederos,* meaning "a child as beautiful as love."

Opal is best worn as a pinkie ring. It is also a popular engagement ring, as it symbolizes faithfulness and effectively brings stability and longevity to relationships. Fire opal is good for business by promoting positive action and prosperity. Hold your opal in your right hand and your wishes will be granted.

Crystal Closure

If you are having a hard time getting away from a relationship that you feel isn't good for you any longer, get closure by wearing morganite until the other person gets the message.

RHODOCHROSITE—ROSE-COLORED ROMANCE

The name simply means "rose-colored," and the color is astounding. This stone seems as if it is lit from within. Rhodochrosite is a love stone that will enable anyone who believes they have never truly felt or experienced real love to find it. I heard and read about some people gleaning much good from it during the aftermath of 9/11. It functions as a heart-chakra opener that brings compassion and expands consciousness. One fascinating legend associated with rhodochrosite is that it can connect you to your soulmate if used in meditation. This is also a crystal that helps with the healing power of forgiveness. It also helps overcome irrationality and can prevent a mental breakdown. However, my favorite feature of rhodochrosite is that it overcomes a poor memory. So, this rose-colored beauty banishes forgetfulness and promotes forgiveness—a nice combination. Healers also work with this stone for respiratory diseases. It has a warm energy that is good for the body.

This striking stone is also invaluable for overcoming fear and paranoia (mental unease). Rhodochrosite abets a more positive worldview. One of the simplest and best aspects of this crystal is that it will help you to sleep more peacefully, shoving apprehension, worry, and woe out of your mind so you can heal body and soul. Your dreams will be positive, too. This is a remarkable stone for affirming the self, allowing absolute self-acceptance and self-forgiveness. Rhodochrosite brings together the spiritual plane and the material place. The crystal is important because it permits the heart to feel hurt and pain deeply, and this processing of emotions nurtures growth.

TOURMALINE—TRUE LOVE

Purple tourmaline is a stone of devotion. Lending the highest spiritual aspirations, this crystal works by connecting the root and heart chakras. It greatly enables the ability to love unconditionally and creatively. Purple tourmaline is a heart healer.

Conclusion

LOVE INTENTIONS

Dear reader, I wish an abundance of love and joy for you. I also suggest you keep a record of your magical workings in a Book of Shadows, your notebook for spellwork. Your Book of Shadows can and should be a document of what works for you in terms of specifics—moon phases, colors, numbers, herbs, etc. You can greatly expand your BOS with notes on your ritual projects and life as a work in progress. Here you should inscribe your musings, your writing of invocations, your hopes, and your intentions. I call this the "journal of the journey," and it can take any form of your imagination as long as it catches the deep truths of what you hope to accomplish.

Your ritual record need not be fancy, but it should be raw, honest, and real. Tell the stories of what *really* happened, mistakes and all. Those who are the most truthful and open will gain the most from their record of experience. Not every group ritual will be a smashing success—someone will be grumpy, someone else might say the words wrong, or you may all get nervous and forget what to do. Or nature may change your plans. For example, an outdoor full moon circle planned for a year may be driven indoors by a rainstorm that puts out candles and wilts every spirit.

Nevertheless, I am always encouraged and amazed to discover the so-called mistakes from which we learn the most. If everything is perfect, the ritual will likely slip from memory. Life itself is messy and bumpy. Think of the metaphor of the Navajo blanked in which the weaver, despite his skill, always makes one mistake. The metaphor is that life itself is not perfect, and the blanket should be reflective of life. That one "crooked thread" can be the strongest stitch holding the fabric of your life together.

Bright blessings and much love to you and yours!

Xoxo

Appendix 1

DATES AND DAYS OF THE WEEK

his section contains lists and tables of information you can use to cast spells and work magic using dates, planets, goals, and astrological signs. (If a date is listed as being both lucky and unlucky, the ritualist is free to make their own decision regarding personal practice.)

Sabbats

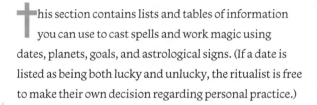

+ + Four Major Sabbats + +	
Candlemas	February
Beltane	May 1
Lammas	August 1
Samhain	October 31

+ + Four Lesser Sabbats + +	
Vernal Equinox	March 20
Summer Solstice	June 24
Autumn Equinox	September 23
Winter Solstice/Yule	December 21

+ + LUCKY AND UNLUCKY DATES + +

January
Lucky Dates: 3, 10, 27, 31
Unlucky Dates: 12, 23

February
Lucky Dates: 7, 8, 18
Unlucky Dates: 2, 10, 17, 22

March
Lucky Dates: 3, 9, 12, 14, 16
Unlucky Dates: 13, 19, 23, 28

April
Lucky Dates: 5, 17
Unlucky Dates: 18, 20, 29, 30

Month: May
Lucky Dates: 1, 2, 4, 6, 9, 14
Unlucky Dates: 10, 17, 20

Month: June
Lucky Dates: 3, 5, 7, 9, 13, 23
Unlucky Dates: 4, 20

Month: July
Lucky Dates: 2, 6, 10, 23, 30
Unlucky Dates: 5, 13, 27

Month: August
Lucky Dates: 5, 7, 10, 14
Unlucky Dates: 2, 13, 27, 31

Month: September
Lucky Dates: 6, 10, 13, 18, 30
Unlucky Dates: 13, 16, 18

Month: October
Lucky Dates: 13, 16, 25, 31
Unlucky Dates: 3, 9, 27

Month: November
Lucky Dates: 1, 13, 23, 30
Unlucky Dates: 6, 25

Month: December
Lucky Dates: 10, 20, 29
Unlucky Dates: 15, 26

✦ DAYS, PLANETS, COLORS, AND GOALS ✦

Day: Sunday
Planet: Sun
Correspondence: Exorcism, healing, prosperity
Color: Orange, white, yellow
Incense: Lemon, frankincense

Day: Monday
Planet: Moon
Correspondence: Agriculture, animals, female fertility, messages, reconciliation, voyages
Color: Silver, white, gray
Incense: African violet, honeysuckle, myrtle, willow, wormwood

Day: Tuesday
Planet: Mars
Correspondence: Courage, physical strength, revenge, military honors, surgery, breaking negative spells
Color: Red, orange
Incense: Dragon's blood, patchouli

Day: Wednesday
Planet: Mercury
Correspondence: Knowledge, communication, divination, writing, business transactions
Color: Yellow, gray, violet, all opalescent hues
Incense: Jasmine, lavender, sweet pea

Day: Thursday
Planet: Jupiter
Correspondence: Luck, health, happiness, legal matters, male fertility, treasure, wealth, employment
Color: Purple, indigo
Incense: Cinnamon, musk, nutmeg, sage

Day: Friday
Planet: Venus
Correspondence: Love, romance, marriage, sexual matters, physical beauty, friendships, partnerships
Color: Pink, green, aqua, chartreuse
Incense: Strawberry, rose, sandalwood, saffron, vanilla

Day: Saturday
Planet: Saturn
Correspondence: Spirit, communication, meditation, psychic attack or defense, locating lost or missing persons
Color: Black, gray, indigo

Appendix II

THE LANGUAGE OF FLOWERS

H ere is what each of the following flowers means so that you can select the right flowers for your ritual.

Abatina: Fickleness

Acacia: Chaste love

Acacia, Pink: Elegance

Acacia, Yellow: Secret love

Aconite, Crowfoot: Lust

Agrimony: Thankfulness, gratitude

Allspice: Compassion

Almond: Stupidity, indiscretion

Almond, Flowering: Hope

Almond, Laurel: Perfidy

Aloe: Grief, affection

Althea Frutex: Persuasion

Alyssum, Sweet: Worth beyond beauty

Amaranth: Immortality, unfading love

Amaranth, Cockscomb: affectation

Amaranth, Globe: Unchangeable

Amaryllis: Pride

Ambrosia: Love returned

American Linden: Matrimony

B

Bachelor's Buttons:
Single blessedness

Balm: Sympathy

Balm, Gentle: Pleasantry

Balm of Gilead: Cure, relief

Balsam, Red: Touch me not,
impatient resolve

Bay Tree: Glory

Bearded Crepis: Protection

Beech Tree: Prosperity

Belladonna: Silence

Betony: Surprise

Birch: Meekness

Bitterweed, Nightshade: Truth

Black Poplar: Courage

C

Cacalia: Adulation

Cactus: Warmth

Calceolaria: Keep this for my sake

Calla Aethiopica:
Magnificent beauty

Calycanthus: Benevolence

Campanula: Gratitude

Canariensis: Self-esteem

Canary Grass: Perseverance

Candytuft: Indifference

Canterbury Bell: Acknowledgment

Cardamine: Paternal error

Catchfly, Red: Youthful love

Cedar: Strength

Cedar Leaf: I live for thee

Celandine: Joys to come

Centaury: Felicity

Crown, Imperial: Majesty, powerful

D

Daffodil: Regard

Daffodil, Great
Yellow: Chivalry

Dahlia: Instability

Dahlia, Single:
Good taste

Daisy, Double:
Participation

Daisy, Garden: I share
your sentiment

Daisy, One-Eyed: A token

Daisy, Party-colored: Beauty

Daisy, Red: Unconscious

Daisy, White: Innocent

Daisy, Wild: I will think of it

Dandelion: Oracle

Daphne Odora: Painting the lily

Darnel: Vice

Dead Leaves: Sadness

Dew Plant: A serenade

Diosma: Uselessness

Dittany, White: Passion

Dittany of Crete: Birth

Dock: Patience

Dodder of Thyme: Baseness

Dogbane: Deceit, falsehood

Dogwood: Durability

Dragon Plant: Snare

Dragonwort: Horror

Dried Flax: Utility

Ebony Tree: Blackness

Eglantine or Sweet Briar: Poetry, I wound to heal

Elder: Zealousness

Elm: Dignity

Enchanter's Nightshade: Fascination, witchcraft

Endive: Frugality

Eschscholtzia: Sweetness

Eupatorium: Delay

Evergreen: Poverty

Evergreen, Thorn: Solace in adversity

Everlasting Pea: Lasting pleasure, an appointed meeting

Fennel: Worthy of all praise

Fern: Sincerity

Fern, Flowering: Fascination

Ficoides, Ice Plant: Your looks freeze me

Fig: Argument

Fig, Marigold: Idleness

Fig Tree: Prolific

Flax: Fate, domestic industry, I feel your kindness

Flax-leaved Golden Locks: Tardiness

Fleur-de-lis: Flame

Fleur-de-Luce: Confidence in heaven

Flower-of-an-Hour: Delicate beauty

Fly Orchis: Error

Fly Trap: Deceit

Fools Parsley: Silliness

Forget-Me-Not: True love

Foxglove: Insincerity

Foxtail Grass: Sporting

French Honeysuckle: Rustic beauty

French Marigold: Jealousy

Frog Ophrys: Disgust

Fritillary, Chequered: Persecution

Fuchsia, Scarlet: Taste

Fullers Teasel: Misanthropy, importunity

Fumitory: Spleen

Furze or Gorse: Enduring affection

G

Garden Anemone: Forsaken

Garden Chervil: Sincerity

Garden Marigold: Uneasiness

Garden Ranunculus: You are rich in attractions

Garden Sage: Esteem

Garland of Roses: Reward of virtue

Gentian: You are unjust

Germander Speedwell: Facility

Geranium, Dark: Melancholy

Geranium, Ivy: Bridal favor

Geranium, Nutmeg: An expected meeting

Geranium, Oak-leaved: True friendship

Geranium, Pencil-leaved: Ingenuity

Geranium, Rose or Pink: Preference

Geranium, Scarlet: Comforting

Geranium, Silver-leaved: Recall

Geranium, Wild: Steadfast piety

Gillyflower: Lasting beauty

Gladiolus: Strength of character

Glory Flower: Glorious beauty

Gloxinia: A proud spirit

Goats Rue: Reason

H

Hand Flower Tree: Warming

Harebell: Submission, grief

Hawkweed: Quick sightedness

Hawthorne: Hope

Hazel: Reconciliation

Heartsease or Pansy: You occupy my thoughts

Heath: Solitude

Helenium: Tears

Heliotrope: Devotion

Hellebore: Scandal, calumny

Hemlock: You will be my death

Hemp: Fate

Henbane: Imperfection

Hepatica: Confidence

Hibiscus: Delicate beauty

Holly: Foresight

Holly Herb: Enchantment

Hollyhock: Fecundity

Honesty: Honesty, sincerity

Honey Flower: Love sweet and secret

Honeysuckle: Bonds of love, sweetness of disposition

Honeysuckle, Coral: The color of my fate

Honeysuckle, French: Rustic beauty

Hop: Injustice

Hornbeam: Ornament

Hortensia: You are cold

Houseleek: Vivacity, domestic economy

Houstonia: Content

Hoya: Sculpture

Humble Plant: Despotism

Hyacinth: Sport, game, play

Hyacinth, Blue: Constancy

Hyacinth, Purple: Sorrow

Hyacinth, White: Unobtrusiveness, loveliness

Hydrangea: A boaster, heartlessness

Hyssop: Cleanliness

Ice Plant: Your looks freeze me

Iceland Moss: Health

Imperial Montaque: Power

Indian Cress: Warlike trophy

Indian Pink, Double: Always lovely

Indian Plum: Privation

Iris: Message

Iris, German: Flame

Ivy: Friendship, fidelity

Ivy, Sprig of with tendrils: Assiduous to please

Jacob's Ladder: Come down

Japan Rose: Beauty is your only attraction

Jasmine, Cape: Transport of joy

Jasmine, Carolina: Separation

Jasmine, Indian: Attachment

Jasmine, Spanish: Sensuality

Jasmine, Yellow: Grace and elegance

Jasmine, White: Amiability

Jonquil: I desire a return of affection

Judas Tree: Unbelief, betrayal

Justicia: The perfection of female loveliness

Kennedya: Mental beauty

Kingcups: Desire of riches

L

Laburnum: Forsaken, pensive beauty

Lady's Slipper: Capricious beauty

Lagerstroemia, Indian: Eloquence

Lantana: Rigor

Larch: Audacity, boldness

Larkspur: Lightness, levity

Larkspur, Pink: Fickleness

Larkspur, Purple: Haughtiness

Laurel: Glory

Laurel, Common in the flower: Perfidy

Laurel, Ground: Perseverance

Laurel, Mountain: Ambition

Laurestina: A token

Lavender: Distrust

Leaves, Dead: Melancholy

Lemon: Zest

Lemon Blossoms: Fidelity in love

Lent Lilly: Sweet disposition

Lettuce: Cold-heartedness

Lichen: Dejection, solitude

Lilac, Field: Humility

Lilac, Purple: First emotions of love

Lilac, White: Youthful innocence

Lily, Day: Coquetry

Lily, Yellow: Falsehood, gaiety

Lilly of the Valley: Return of happiness

Linden or Lime Tree: Conjugal love

Lint: I feel my obligation

Liquorice, Wild: I declare against you

Live Oak: Liberty

Liverwort: Confidence

Lobelia: Malevolence

Locust Tree: Elegance

Locust Tree, Green: Affection beyond the grave

London Pride: Frivolity

Lote Tree: Concord

Lotus: Eloquence

Lotus Flower: Estranged love

Lotus Leaf: Recantation

Love-in-a-Mist: Perplexity

Love-Lies-Bleeding: Hopeless, not heartless

Lucerne: Life

Lupin: Voraciousness

Madder: Calumny

Magnolia: Love of nature

Magnolia, Laurel-leaved: Dignity

Magnolia, Swamp: Perseverance

Mallow: Mildness

Mallow, Marsh: Beneficence

Mallow, Syrian: Consumed by love

Mallow, Venetian: Delicate beauty

Manchineel Tree: Falsehood

Mandrake: Horror

Maple: Reserve

Marigold: Grief, despair

Marigold, African: Vulgar minds

Marigold, French: Jealousy

Marigold, Prophetic: Prediction

Marjoram: Blushes

Marvel of Peru: Timidity

Meadow Lychnis: Wit

Meadow Saffron: My best days are past

Meadowsweet: Uselessness

Mercury: Goodness

Mesembryanthemum: Idleness

Mezereon: Desire to please

Michaelmas Daisy: Afterthought

Mignonette: Your qualities surpass your charms

Milfoil: War

Milkvetch: Your presence softens my pains

Milkwort: Hermitage

Mimosa, Sensitive Plant: Sensitiveness

Mint: Virtue

Mistletoe: I surmount difficulties

Narcissus, Double: Female ambition

Nasturtium: Patriotism

Nemophila: I forgive you

Nettle, Common Stinging: You are cruel

Nettle, Burning: Slander

Night-blooming Cereus: Transient beauty

Night Convolvulus: Night

Nightshade: Falsehood

O

Oak Leaves: Bravery

Oak Tree: Hospitality

Oats: The witching soul of music

Oleander: Beware

Olive: Peace

N

Narcissus: Egotism

Orange Blossoms: Bridal festivities, your purity equals your loveliness

Orange Flowers: Chastity

Orange Tree: Generosity

Orchid: A belle

Osier: Frankness

Osmunda: Dreams

Ox Eye: Patience

Quaking Grass: Agitation

Quamoclit: Busybody

Queen's Rocket: You are the Queen of Coquettes, passion

Quince: Temptation

Palm: Victory

Pansy: Thoughts

Parsley: Festivity

Pasque Flower: You have no claims

Passionflower: Religious superstition

Patience Dock: Patience

Pea, Everlasting: An appointed meeting, lasting pleasure

Pea, Sweet: Departure, lasting pleasures

Peach: Your qualities like your charms are unequaled

Peach Blossom: I am your captive

Ragged Robin: Wit

Ranunculus: You are radiant with charms

Ranunculus, Garden: You are rich in all relations

Ranunculus, Wild: Ingratitude

Raspberry: Remorse

Red Catchfly: Youthful love

Reed: Complaisance, music

Reed, Split: Indiscretion

Rhododendron, Rosebay: Danger, beware

Rhubarb: Advice

Rocket: Rivalry

Rye Grass, Darnel: Vice

S

Saffron: Beware of success

Saffron, Crocus: Mirth

Saffron, Meadow: My happiest days are past

Sage: Domestic virtue

Sage, Garden: Esteem

Sainfoin: Agitation

Saint John's Wort: Animosity

Salvia, Blue: I think of you

Salvia, Red: Forever thine

Saxifrage, Mossy: Affection

Scabious: Unfortunate love

Scarlet Lychnis: Sunbeaming eyes

Schinus: Religious enthusiasm

Scilla, Blue: Forgive and forget

Scilla, Sibirica: Pleasure without alloy

Scilla, White: Sweet innocence

Scotch, Fir: Elevation

Sensitive Plant: Sensibility

Shamrock: Light-heartedness

Snakesfoot: Horror

Snowball: Bound

Snowdragon: Presumption

Snowdrop: Hope

Sorrel: Affection

Sorrel, Wild: Wit, ill-timed

Sorrel, Wood: Joy

Stephanotis: You can boast too much

Stock, Ten Week: Promptness

Stonecrop: Tranquility

Straw, Broken: Rupture of a contract

Straw, Whole: Union

Strawberry Blossom: Foresight

Strawberry Tree: Esteem, not love

Sumach, Venice: Splendor

Sunflower, Dwarf: Adoration

Sunflower, Tall: Haughtiness

T

Tamarisk: Crime

Tansy, Wild: I declare war against you

Teasel: Misanthropy

Tendrils of Climbing Plants: Ties

Thistle, Common: Austerity

Thistle, Scotch: Retaliation

Thorn, Apple: Deceitful, charms

Thorns, Branch of: Severity

Thrift: Sympathy

Throatwort: Neglected beauty

Thyme: Activity

Tiger Flower: For once may pride befriend me

Traveler's Joy: Safety

Tree of Life: Old age

Trefoil: Revenge

Tremella: Resistance

Trillium Pictum: Modest beauty

Truffle: Surprise

Tulip, Red: Declaration of love

Tulip, Variegated: Beautiful eyes

Tulip, Yellow: Hopeless love

Turnip: Charity

Tussilago, Sweet-scented: Justice shall be done you

Venus Trap: Deceit

Venus's Car: Fly with me

Venus's Looking Glass: Flattery

Verbena, Scarlet: Sensibility

Verbena, White: Pure and guileless

Vernal Grass: Poor but happy

Veronica: Fidelity

Vervain: Enchantment

Vine: Intoxication

Violet, Blue: Faithfulness

Violet, Dame: Watchfulness

Violet, Sweet: Modesty

Violet, Yellow: Rural happiness

Virginia Creeper: Ever changing

Virgin's Bower: Filial love

Volkmannia: May you be happy

Wallflower: Fidelity in adversity

Walnut: Intellect, stratagem

Water Lily: Purity of heart

Watermelon: Bulkiness

Wax Plant: Susceptibility

Weigela: Accept a faithful heart

Wheat Stalk: Riches

Valerian: An accommodating disposition

Valerian, Greek: Rupture

Whin: Anger

White Jasmine: Amiability

White Lily: Purity and modesty

White Mullein: Good nature

White Oak: Independent

Whortleberry: Treason

Willow, Creeping: Love forsaken

Willow, Water: Freedom

Willow, Weeping: Mourning

Willow, Herb: Pretension

Willow, French: Bravery, humanity

Wisteria: I cling to thee

Witch Hazel: A spell

Woodbine: Fraternal love

Zephyr Flower: Expectation

Zinnia: Thoughts of absent friends

Xanthium: Rudeness, pertinacity

Xeranthemum: Cheerfulness
under adversity

Yew: Sorrow

About the Author

Cerridwen Greenleaf has worked with many of the leading lights of the spiritual world, including Starhawk, Z Budapest, John Michael Greer, Christopher Penczak, Raymond Buckland, Luisah Teish, and many more. She gives herbal workshops throughout North America. Greenleaf's graduate work in medieval studies has given her deep knowledge she utilizes in her work, making her writings unique in the field. Her Witch's Spellbook series are bestsellers. Make sure to check out her inspiring blogs below.

- witchesandpagans.com/pagan-culture-blogs/
  middle-earth-magic.html

- yourmagicalhome.blogspot.com

Mango Publishing, established in 2014, publishes an eclectic list of books by diverse authors—both new and established voices—on topics ranging from business, personal growth, women's empowerment, LGBTQ+ studies, health, and spirituality to history, popular culture, time management, decluttering, lifestyle, mental wellness, aging, and sustainable living. We were recently named 2019 *and* 2020's #1 fastest-growing independent publisher by *Publishers Weekly.* Our success is driven by our main goal, which is to publish high-quality books that will entertain readers as well as make a positive difference in their lives.

Our readers are our most important resource; we value your input, suggestions, and ideas. We'd love to hear from you—after all, we are publishing books for you!

Please stay in touch with us and follow us at:

Facebook: Mango Publishing
Twitter: @MangoPublishing
Instagram: @MangoPublishing
LinkedIn: Mango Publishing
Pinterest: Mango Publishing
Newsletter: mangopublishinggroup.com/newsletter

Join us on Mango's journey to reinvent publishing, one book at a time.